Speaking and Listening 4

Developing children's listening skills
in the daily maths lesson

Peter Clarke

William Collins' dream of knowledge for all began with the publication of his first book in 1819. A self-educated mill worker, he not only enriched millions of lives, but also founded a flourishing publishing house. Today, staying true to this spirit, Collins books are packed with inspiration, innovation and practical expertise. They place you at the centre of a world of possibility and give you exactly what you need to explore it.

Collins. Freedom to teach.

Published by Collins
An imprint of HarperCollins*Publishers* Ltd.
77-85 Fulham Palace Road
Hammersmith
London
W6 8JB

Browse the complete Collins catalogue at
www.collinseducation.com

© HarperCollins*Publishers* Ltd 2009

10 9 8 7

ISBN: 978-0-00-732282-4

Peter Clarke asserts his moral right to be identified as the author of this work.

Any educational institution that has purchased one copy of this publication may make unlimited duplicate copies for use exclusively within that institution. Permission does not extend to reproduction, storage within a retrieval system, or transmittal in any form or by any means, electronic, mechanical, photocopying, recording or otherwise, of duplicate copies for loaning, renting or selling to any other institution without the permission of the Publisher.

British Library Cataloguing in Publication Data
A Catalogue record for this publication is available from the British Library.

Cover template: Laing&Carroll
Cover illustration: Jonatronix Ltd.
Series design: Neil Adams
Illustrations: Roy Mitchell, Bethan Matthews, Jeffrey Reid, Lisa Williams, Mel Sharp, Rhiannon Powell

Acknowledgement
The author wishes to thank Brian Molyneaux for his valuable contribution to this publication.

Printed and bound by Martins the Printers Ltd

FSC is a non-profit international organisation established to promote the responsible management of the world's forests. Products carrying the FSC label are independently certified to assure consumers that they come from forests that are managed to meet the social, economic and ecological needs of present and future generations.

Find out more about HarperCollins and the environment at
www.harpercollins.co.uk/green

Contents

Introduction 4
Listening and communicating 4
Communication and mental imagery 4
The skills of listening 5
Becoming a good listener 5
Characteristics of a good listener 5
Collins New Primary Maths: Speaking and Listening and the teaching–learning cycle 7
Curriculum information 7
Planning a programme of work for *Collins New Primary Maths: Speaking and Listening* 7
Collins New Primary Maths: Speaking and Listening and the daily mathematics lesson 7
Collins New Primary Maths: Speaking and Listening objectives coverage 8
Collins New Primary Maths: Speaking and Listening programme 9
How to use *Collins New Primary Maths: Speaking and Listening* 10
Collins New Primary Maths: Speaking and Listening and assessment 10
Collins New Primary Maths: Speaking and Listening assessment sheet 11

The activities 12
Strand 1: Using and applying mathematics 12
Strand 2: Counting and understanding number 16
Strand 3: Knowing and using number facts 28
Strand 4: Calculating 36
Strand 5: Understanding shape 54
Strand 6: Measuring 58
Strand 7: Handling data 70

Introduction

Collins New Primary Maths: Speaking and Listening is a series of seven books from Foundation to Year 6 which is designed to assist children in practising and consolidating objectives from the *Renewed Primary Framework for Mathematics* (2006) at the same time as developing their listening skills.

Listening and following instructions are two key skills that are crucial to the success of every child and every adult. How many times have children had to redo work because they have not listened to your directions? How many times do you have to repeat yourself? How often have you wished you could take time out from the overburdened curriculum to help children develop their listening skills? This series will help you solve these problems. You will not have to take time away from other curriculum areas to do this since *Collins New Primary Maths: Speaking and Listening* helps to develop children's listening skills and ability to follow oral directions while they practise valuable mathematical skills.

Listening and communicating

The purpose of this book is the development of children's listening skills through the mathematics curriculum, but this skill is not seen in isolation. Many of the activities outlined include reading, speaking and writing. Listening is an integral part of communication which deals with the process of giving and receiving information. The four different aspects of the communication process outlined below rely upon each other for effective communication at the same time as actively supporting and enriching one another.

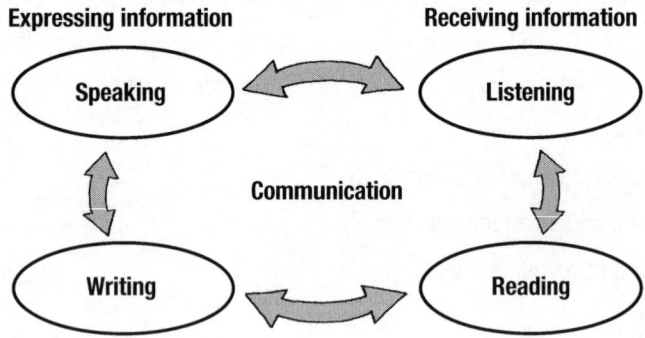

Communication and mental imagery

All children, whatever their age and ability, have their own mental images, developed from previous knowledge and experiences. Aural stimulus enables children to manipulate the mental images they have of numbers, shapes and measures. Instant recall of number facts such as the multiplication tables and the addition and subtraction number facts often depends on an aural input. Children have to hear the sounds in order to give an automatic response.

The difficult part for the teacher is to discover what is going on inside children's heads. This is where discussion as an accompaniment to mental work is so important. It is only through discussion that the teacher can begin to develop an insight into children's mental processes. Discussions also enable children to develop their own insights into their mental imagery and provide the opportunity for them to share their ideas and methods. They can form judgements about the alternatives, decide which methods are the most efficient and effective for them, and further develop flexibility and familiarity with the different mathematical topics.

The skills of listening

Listening skills can be improved through training and practice. When direct attention is paid to listening for specific purposes, and these skills are practised and consolidated, improvement in ability follows. In general children tend to learn and remember more through listening than in almost any other way. A high percentage of all the information children receive comes through their ears. Thus direct training in the skills of listening can be hugely beneficial to all learning.

Effective listening involves:
- hearing
- concentrating
- a knowledge of language
- a knowledge of the structure of language
- recognising cues
- being able to contextualise
- inferring
- thinking
- processing
- summarising
- selecting
- organising
- drawing upon previous knowledge and experience
- comprehending/understanding the main idea.

Becoming a good listener

Display the poster on page 6 to remind children of how to become a good listener. When concentrating on developing children's listening skills draw attention to the poster.

Characteristics of a good listener

A good listener is one who:
- knows how to listen
- is able to concentrate on listening
- looks at the speaker
- is courteous to the speaker
- does not interrupt the speaker
- is able to zero in on the speaker and eliminate extraneous noises and interruptions
- can comprehend
- is selective
- asks him/herself questions while listening
- draws upon their previous knowledge and experiences
- evaluates while listening
- remembers what is said
- anticipates what is coming next.

Good listening

Sit still

Think about the words

Look at the speaker

Collins New Primary Maths: Speaking and Listening and the teaching–learning cycle

Assessment
- Each activity can be used to assess a specific objective from the *Renewed Primary Framework for Mathematics* (2006).
- Guidance given on how to record pupil performance.

Planning
- Each activity linked to an objective in the *Renewed Primary Framework for Mathematics* (2006)
- Guidance given for planning a programme of work.

Teaching
- Clear and complete instructions given for each activity.
- Ideally suited to the daily mathematics lesson.

Curriculum information

Each of the 30 activities is organised under specific objectives as identified in the *Renewed Primary Framework for Mathematics* (2006). The *Collins New Primary Maths: Speaking and Listening* objectives coverage chart on page 8 shows which activity is matched to which objective(s).

Planning a programme of work for *Collins New Primary Maths: Speaking and Listening*

The *Collins New Primary Maths: Speaking and Listening* programme chart on page 9 may be used in conjunction with your long- and medium-term plans to develop a *Collins New Primary Maths: Speaking and Listening* programme of work throughout the year. By following the Blocks and Units from the *Renewed Primary Framework for Mathematics* (2006) you will ensure that the children have the opportunity to practise and consolidate the strands, and specific objectives for a particular unit of work, at the same time as developing their listening skills.

Collins New Primary Maths: Speaking and Listening and the daily mathematics lesson

The activities contained in *Collins New Primary Maths: Speaking and Listening* are ideally suited to the daily mathematics lesson. Each activity is designed to be presented to the whole class. The activities are extremely flexible and can be used in a variety of ways. For example, activities can be used during the:
- oral work and mental calculation session to practise and consolidate previously taught concepts;
- main teaching part of the lesson to focus on particular skills and concepts;
- plenary session to consolidate the concept(s) taught during the main part of the lesson and to conclude the lesson in an enjoyable way.

Collins New Primary Maths: Speaking and Listening objectives coverage

STRAND	OBJECTIVES	ACTIVITY	PAGE
1: Using and applying mathematics	Solve one-step and two-step problems involving numbers; choose and carry out appropriate calculations, using calculator methods where appropriate.	1	12
	Solve one-step and two-step problems involving money; choose and carry out appropriate calculations, using calculator methods where appropriate.	2	14
2: Counting and understanding number	(Read and write whole numbers to at least 10 000.) Partition four-digit whole numbers.	3	16
	Order four-digit whole numbers; state inequalities using the symbols < and >. (Give one or more numbers lying between two given numbers.)	4	18
	Round (two-digit and three-digit) whole numbers.	5	20
	Recognise and continue number sequences formed by counting on or back in steps of constant size (extending beyond zero when counting back).	6	22
	Identify equivalent fractions; interpret mixed numbers.	7	24
	Use decimal notation for tenths and hundredths and partition decimals; relate the notation to money.	8	26
3: Knowing and using number facts	Use knowledge of addition and subtraction facts (to 20) and place value to derive sums and differences (including pairs that total 100 and pairs of multiples of 50 that total 1000).	9	28
	Derive and recall multiplication facts up to 10 × 10.	10	30
	Derive and recall division facts corresponding to the 2, 3, 4, 5 and 10 times-tables.	11	32
	Identify the doubles of two-digit numbers; use these to calculate doubles of multiples of 10 and 100 and derive the corresponding halves.	12	34
4: Calculating	Add or subtract mentally pairs of two-digit whole numbers.	13	36
	Refine and use efficient written methods to add two-digit and three-digit whole numbers (and more than two whole numbers).	14	38
	Refine and use efficient written methods to add and subtract two-digit and three-digit whole numbers.	15	40
	Refine and use efficient written methods to add and subtract two-digit and three-digit whole numbers and £.p.	16	42
	Multiply and divide numbers to 1000 by 10 and then 100 (whole-number answers), understanding the effect; relate to scaling up or down. (Add and subtract 1, 10, 100 and 1000 to or from any whole number.)	17	44
	Multiply and divide numbers to 1000 by 10 and then 100 (whole-number answers), understanding the effect; relate to scaling up or down. **Derive and recall multiplication facts up to 10 × 10, the corresponding division facts and multiples of numbers to 10 up to the tenth multiple.**	18	46
	Develop and use written methods to record, support and explain multiplication of two-digit numbers by a one-digit number.	19	48
	Develop and use written methods to record, support and explain division of two-digit numbers by a one-digit number, including division with remainders.	20	50
	Develop and use written methods to record, support and explain division of two-digit numbers by a one-digit number, including division with remainders.	21	52
5: Understanding shape	Draw polygons and classify them by identifying their properties, including their line symmetry. Visualise 3-D objects from 2-D drawings.	22	54
	Use the eight compass points to describe direction.	23	56
6: Measuring	**Choose and use standard metric units and their abbreviations when estimating, measuring and recording length.** Solve one-step and two-step problems involving measures.	24	58
	Choose and use standard metric units and their abbreviations when estimating, measuring and recording mass. Solve one-step and two-step problems involving measures.	25	60
	Choose and use standard metric units and their abbreviations when estimating, measuring and recording capacity. Solve one-step and two-step problems involving measures.	26	62
	Draw rectangles and measure and calculate their perimeters; find the area of rectilinear shapes drawn on a square grid by counting squares.	27	64
	Read time to the nearest minute; use am, pm and 12-hour clock notation.	28	66
	Calculate time intervals using a calendar.	29	68
7: Handling data	**Answer a question by identifying what data to collect; organise, present, analyse and interpret the data in diagrams** (e.g. Venn and Carroll diagrams).	30	70

Key objectives are in bold.

Collins New Primary Maths: Speaking and Listening programme

YEAR
CLASS
TEACHER

	UNIT	MATHEMATICS STRANDS	CNPM: SPEAKING AND LISTENING ACTIVITY
AUTUMN	A1	**Counting, partitioning and calculating** Strand 1: Using and applying mathematics Strand 2: Counting and understanding number Strand 3: Knowing and using number facts Strand 4: Calculating	
	B1	**Securing number facts, understanding shapes** Strand 1: Using and applying mathematics Strand 3: Knowing and using number facts Strand 5: Understanding shape	
	C1	**Handling data and measures** Strand 1: Using and applying mathematics Strand 6: Measuring Strand 7: Handling data	
	D1	**Calculating, measuring and understanding shape** Strand 1: Using and applying mathematics Strand 4: Calculating Strand 5: Understanding shape Strand 6: Measuring	
	E1	**Securing number facts, calculating, identifying relationships** Strand 1: Using and applying mathematics Strand 2: Counting and understanding number Strand 3: Knowing and using number facts Strand 4: Calculating	
SPRING	A2	**Counting, partitioning and calculating** Strand 1: Using and applying mathematics Strand 2: Counting and understanding number Strand 3: Knowing and using number facts Strand 4: Calculating	
	B2	**Securing number facts, understanding shapes** Strand 1: Using and applying mathematics Strand 3: Knowing and using number facts Strand 5: Understanding shape	
	C2	**Handling data and measures** Strand 1: Using and applying mathematics Strand 6: Measuring Strand 7: Handling data	
	D2	**Calculating, measuring and understanding shape** Strand 1: Using and applying mathematics Strand 4: Calculating Strand 5: Understanding shape Strand 6: Measuring	
	E2	**Securing number facts, calculating, identifying relationships** Strand 1: Using and applying mathematics Strand 2: Counting and understanding number Strand 3: Knowing and using number facts Strand 4: Calculating	
SUMMER	A3	**Counting, partitioning and calculating** Strand 1: Using and applying mathematics Strand 2: Counting and understanding number Strand 3: Knowing and using number facts Strand 4: Calculating	
	B3	**Securing number facts, understanding shapes** Strand 1: Using and applying mathematics Strand 3: Knowing and using number facts Strand 5: Understanding shape	
	C3	**Handling data and measures** Strand 1: Using and applying mathematics Strand 6: Measuring Strand 7: Handling data	
	D3	**Calculating, measuring and understanding shape** Strand 1: Using and applying mathematics Strand 4: Calculating Strand 5: Understanding shape Strand 6: Measuring	
	E3	**Securing number facts, calculating, identifying relationships** Strand 1: Using and applying mathematics Strand 2: Counting and understanding number Strand 3: Knowing and using number facts Strand 4: Calculating	

How to use Collins New Primary Maths: Speaking and Listening

Preparation
- Provide each child with the necessary resources. These can be found at the beginning of each activity's teacher's page.

Instructions
Explain the following to the children:
- They need to listen carefully.
- They will be given some oral instructions to follow.
- The instructions will only be given once.
- They must only do what they are told to do, nothing more.
- They may not use an eraser.
- How many instructions there are for the particular activity.
- That they are to do each task immediately after the instructions for that part have been given.

The activity
- If necessary, briefly discuss the pupil sheet with the children. Ensure that the children are familiar with the pictures and/or the text on the sheet.
- Ensure that the children are also familiar with any of the terms used in the oral instructions. Refer to the *Key words* for a list of the relevant vocabulary.
- Ask the children to write the date on the sheet in the space provided.
- Do not ask the children to write their name. This will occur during the activity.
- Slowly read the instructions to the children.

Discussion
- After the children have completed the sheet, discuss the activity with the class. You may decide to do this either before or after marking the activity. Use the *Discussion questions* as a springboard. For each activity there are questions that have been designed to cater for higher attaining (↑) and lower attaining (↓) pupils.

Marking
- Mark the sheet with the whole class, either before or after the discussion. You may wish the children to mark their own sheet or to swap with someone next to them. However, if you are using the activity as an assessment tool then you may decide to mark the sheets yourself at a later stage.

Revisiting an activity
- Repeat an activity with the class at a later stage in the year. Children can compare how they performed on the task the second time round.
- You may like to alter the activity slightly by changing one or two of the instructions.

Collins New Primary Maths: Speaking and Listening and assessment

Collins New Primary Maths: Speaking and Listening activities may be used with the whole class or with groups of children as an assessment activity. Linked to the topic that is being studied at present, *Collins New Primary Maths: Speaking and Listening* will provide you with an indication of how well the children have understood the objectives being covered as well as how their listening skills are developing. The *Collins New Primary Maths: Speaking and Listening* assessment sheet on page 11 may be used to record how well the children have understood the objectives covered in the activity.

Collins New Primary Maths: Speaking and Listening assessment sheet

| YEAR |
| CLASS |
| TEACHER |

/ Not understood   ∠ Developing an understanding   △ Completely understood

NAME	\\multicolumn{30}{c	}{ACTIVITY}
	1	2	3	4	5	6	7	8	9	10	11	12	13	14	15	16	17	18	19	20	21	22	23	24	25	26	27	28	29	30

Collins New Primary Maths: Speaking and Listening 4 © HarperCollins*Publishers* Ltd 2009

Activity 1

Year 4 Using and applying mathematics

- Solve one-step and two-step problems involving numbers; choose and carry out appropriate calculations, using calculator methods where appropriate.

Resources
Provide each child with the following:
- a copy of Activity 1 pupil sheet
- a coloured pencil
- a pencil

Key words
add   addition   plus   sum   total   more than   subtraction
subtract   take away   minus   difference   less than   multiplication
multiply   times   lots of   groups of   division   divide by
half/halve/one quarter   equals   altogether

Say to the children:
Listen carefully.
I am going to tell you some things to do.
I will say them only once, so listen very carefully.
Do only the things you are told to do and nothing else.
If you make a mistake, cross it out. Do not use an eraser.
There are 14 parts to this activity.

The activity

1. Write your name at the top of the sheet.
2. This activity is similar to Bingo. Using your coloured pencil, colour any four numbers on the sheet. These are your bingo numbers.
   I am going to read out some word problems. You have to work out the answer. If the answer is one of your bingo numbers, draw a cross through that number. If the answer is not one of your bingo numbers write the answer in the waste paper basket. When you have crossed out all four of your coloured numbers, call out 'Bingo!'
3. Question 1 – I think of a number, then add 16. The answer is 34. What was my number?
4. Question 2 – A car has four wheels. How many wheels have 12 cars?
5. Question 3 – A car has four wheels and a motor cycle has two wheels. How many wheels have seven cars and eight motor cycles?
6. Question 4 – Marcel has 38 toy cars. Louisa has half as many. How many toy cars has Louisa?
7. Question 5 – A bucket holds 80 tennis balls. How many are left in the bucket if Tim hits 17 balls?
8. Question 6 – A box holds 70 sweets. How many children can have five sweets each?
9. Question 7 – A crate holds 50 cartons of milk. How many cartons of milk are there in seven crates?
10. Question 8 – A box holds 60 bananas. How many boxes are needed to hold 300 bananas?
11. Question 9 – I think of a number, add three, then multiply by four. The answer is 20. What was my number?
12. Question 10 – There are 128 children in the hall. Another 63 join them. Then 90 leave. How many children are left in the hall?
13. Question 11 – A classroom has six groups. Three groups have five children in each. Two groups have six children in each. One group has four children. How many children are in the class altogether?
14. Question 12 – There are 48 people at the swimming baths. Half of them are in the big pool. One quarter of them are in the small pool. How many people are in both pools altogether?

*Continue until a child has crossed out all four of their numbers and has called out 'Bingo!' Check the child's sheet with the answers above.
If time allows continue until you have read out all 12 questions.*

Answers

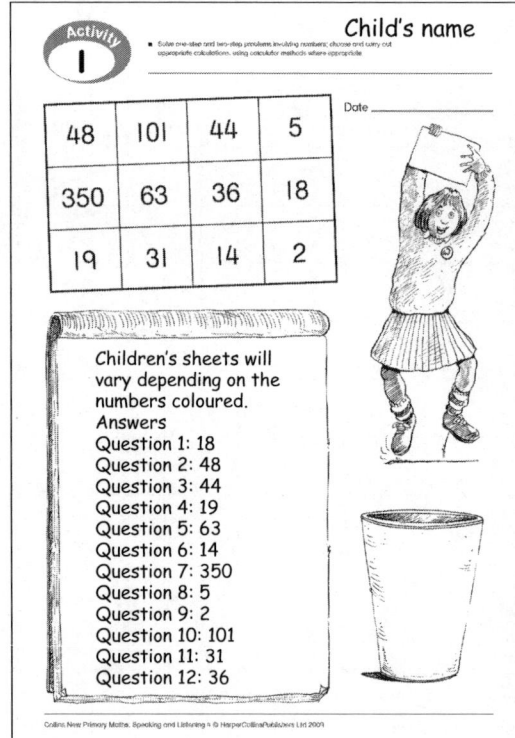

Children's sheets will vary depending on the numbers coloured.
Answers
Question 1: 18
Question 2: 48
Question 3: 44
Question 4: 19
Question 5: 63
Question 6: 14
Question 7: 350
Question 8: 5
Question 9: 2
Question 10: 101
Question 11: 31
Question 12: 36

Discussion questions

- ↓ How many of your bingo numbers did you cross out?
- ↓ Tell me one of the bingo numbers you crossed out.
- ■ Look at your working out. Choose a calculation you worked out and explain what you did.
- ■ Did you find this activity easy or hard? Why?
- ↑ Question 9 was: I think of a number, add three, then multiply by four. The answer was? (2) How did you work it out? Did anyone work it out a different way?
- ↑ Choose one of the numbers you did not colour and put it into a word problem.

Activity 1

- Solve one-step and two-step problems involving numbers; choose and carry out appropriate calculations, using calculator methods where appropriate.

Date _____

48	101	44	5
350	63	36	18
19	31	14	2

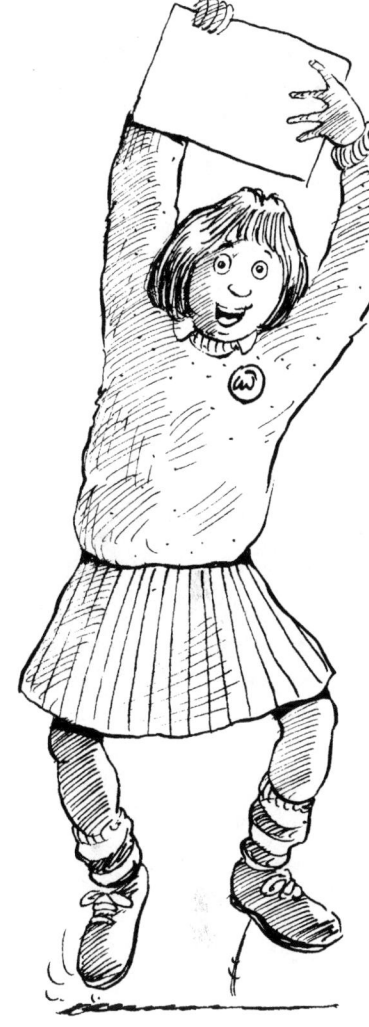

Working out

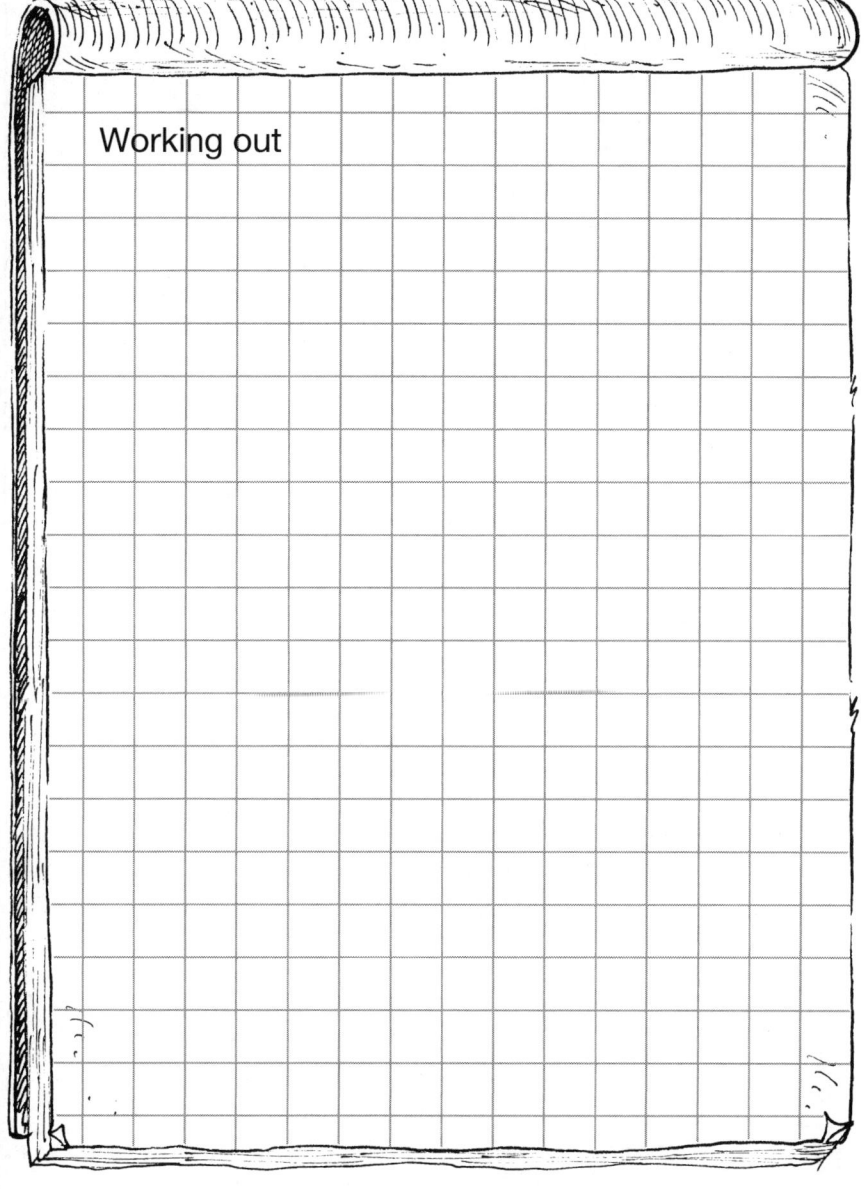

Collins New Primary Maths: Speaking and Listening 4 © HarperCollinsPublishers Ltd 2009

Activity 2

Year 4 Using and applying mathematics

- Solve one-step and two-step problems involving money; choose and carry out appropriate calculations, using calculator methods where appropriate.

Resources
Provide each child with the following:
- a copy of Activity 2 pupil sheet
- a coloured pencil
- a pencil

Key words
add   addition   plus   sum   total   more than   subtraction   subtract   take away   minus   difference   less than   multiplication   multiply   times   lots of   groups of   division   divide by   half/halve/one quarter   equals   altogether   cost   change   pounds/pence

Say to the children:
Listen carefully.
I am going to tell you some things to do.
I will say them only once, so listen very carefully.
Do only the things you are told to do and nothing else.
If you make a mistake, cross it out. Do not use an eraser.
There are 14 parts to this activity.

The activity

1. Write your name at the bottom of the sheet.
2. This activity is similar to Bingo. Using your coloured pencil, colour any four labels on the sheet. These are your bingo numbers. I am going to read out some word problems. You have to work out the answer. If the answer is one of your bingo numbers, draw a cross through that label. If the answer is not one of your bingo numbers write the answer in the carrier bag. When you have crossed out all four of your numbers call out 'Bingo!'
3. Question 1 – What is the total cost of a £2.70 sandwich and a £1.10 drink?
4. Question 2 – A bag of apples costs 80p. How much does it cost for seven bags of apples?
5. Question 3 – Joy has three 50p coins and four 20p coins. She pays £1.30 for her school dinner. How much money does she have left?
6. Question 4 – Petrol costs 73p a litre. What do you pay to fill a five litre can?
7. Question 5 – Four people paid £68 for theatre tickets. What was the cost of each ticket?
8. Question 6 – What change do you get from £10 for £7.39?
9. Question 7 – Chews cost five for £1. How much does one chew cost?
10. Question 8 – Write 840p in pounds and pence.
11. Question 9 – A sports store is having a half price sale. If a pair of trainers were £47 before the sale, how much do they cost in the sale?
12. Question 10 – How many pence is £1.07?
13. Question 11 – David spent one quarter of his money on a CD. What did the CD cost if he had £10?
14. Question 12 – What is the total of £3.40, £2.30 and £1.35?

Continue until a child has crossed out all four of their numbers and has called out 'Bingo!' Check the child's sheet with the answers above. If time allows, continue until you have read out all 12 questions.

Answers

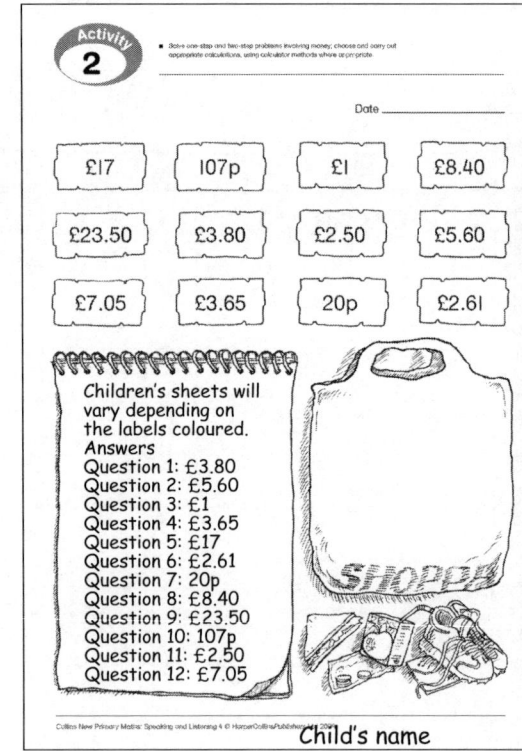

Discussion questions

↓ How many of your labels did you cross out?
↓ Tell me one of the labels you crossed out.
■ Look at your working out. Choose a calculation you worked out and explain what you did.
■ Did you find this activity easy or hard? What was easy/hard about it? Which calculations do you find easy/hard? Why do you think this is so?
↑ Question four was 'Petrol costs 73p a litre. What do you pay to fill a five litre can?' What was the answer? (£3.65) How did you work it out? Did anyone work it out a different way?
↑ Choose one of the labels you did not colour and put it into a word problem.

- Solve one-step and two-step problems involving money; choose and carry out appropriate calculations, using calculator methods where appropriate.

Date _____

£17	107p	£1	£8.40
£23.50	£3.80	£2.50	£5.60
£7.05	£3.65	20p	£2.61

Working out

Year 4 Counting and understanding number

- (Read and write whole numbers to at least 10 000.)
- Partition four-digit whole numbers.

Resources
Provide each child with the following:
- a copy of Activity 3 pupil sheet
- a pencil

Key words
zero, one, two…ten thousand calculation number figures words represent thousands hundreds tens units (ones) square circle triangle rectangle star first, second, third, fourth

Say to the children:
Listen carefully.
I am going to tell you some things to do.
I will say them only once, so listen very carefully.
Do only the things you are told to do and nothing else.
If you make a mistake, cross it out. Do not use an eraser.
There are 14 parts to this activity.

The activity

1. Look at the tickets. Find the ticket with 4716 on it. Draw a ring around that number.
2. Find the ticket with 4007 on it. Draw a cross through that number.
3. Find the ticket with 4186 on it. Write your name above that number.
4. Look at calculation one. Fill in the missing number.
5. Look at calculation two. Fill in the missing number.
6. Look at calculation four. Fill in the missing number.
7. Look at the shapes. In the circle, write the number 7409 in figures.
8. In the square, write the number that is equivalent to two thousands, seven hundreds, nine tens and three units in figures.
9. In the triangle, write the number 5814 in figures.
10. In the rectangle, write the number 3070 in words.
11. Look at the tickets again. Find the ticket with 4081 on it. What does the digit eight represent? Write this number on the first star.
12. Find the ticket with 445 on it. What does the digit five represent? Write this number on the second star.
13. Find the ticket with 4186 on it. What does the digit one represent? Write this number on the third star.
14. Find the ticket with 4007 on it. What does the digit four represent? Write this number on the fourth star.

Answers

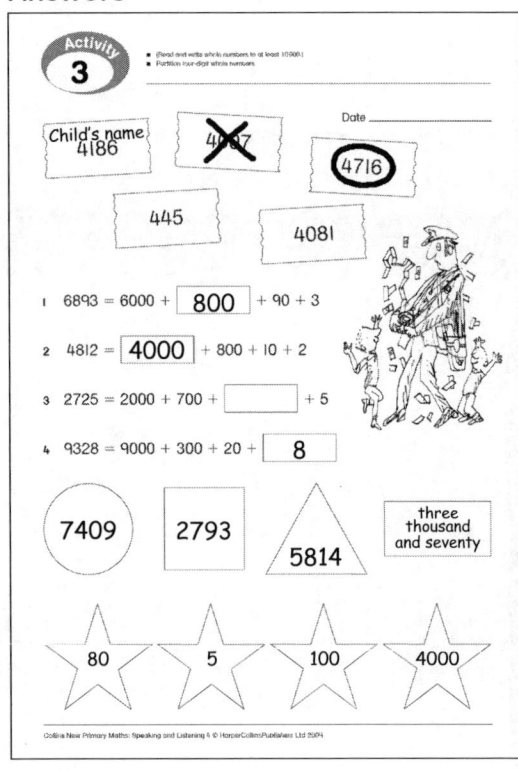

Discussion questions

↓ Look at the tickets. Which number did you draw a cross through? (4007)
↓ Look at calculation two. What does the four represent in 4812? (4000 or 4 thousands) Did you write four thousand in the box?
■ Look at calculation three. Which number should go in the box? (20) Did anyone fill in the box? Were you told to? (no)
■ Look at the numbers on the tickets. Choose a number and write it on the board in words.
↑ Look at the four numbers you have written in the stars. What do these numbers add up to? (4185) Come and write this number on the board in figures/words. (4185/four thousand, one hundred and eighty-five)
↑ Look at the number in the triangle. How many thousands/hundreds/tens/units are in this number? (5/8/1/4)

Activity 3

- (Read and write whole numbers to at least 10 000.)
- Partition four-digit whole numbers.

Date _____

4186   4007   4716

445   4081

1. $6893 = 6000 + \boxed{} + 90 + 3$

2. $4812 = \boxed{} + 800 + 10 + 2$

3. $2725 = 2000 + 700 + \boxed{} + 5$

4. $9328 = 9000 + 300 + 20 + \boxed{}$

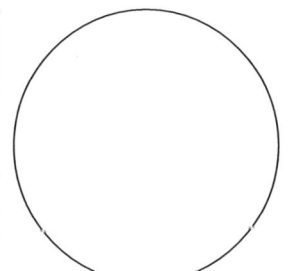  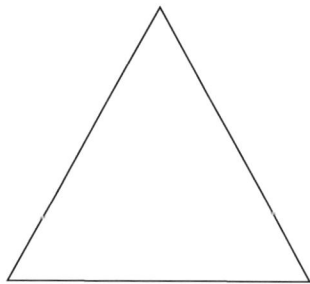 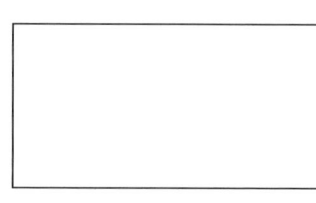

Collins New Primary Maths: Speaking and Listening 4 © HarperCollins*Publishers* Ltd 2009

Year 4 Counting and understanding number

- Order four-digit whole numbers; state inequalities using the symbols < and >.
- (Give one or more numbers lying between two given numbers.)

Resources
Provide each child with the following:
- a copy of Activity 4 pupil sheet
- a pencil

Key words
zero, one, two…ten thousand   less than   fewer than   more than   greater than   statement   true   first   second   smallest   largest

Say to the children:
Listen carefully.
I am going to tell you some things to do.
I will say them only once, so listen very carefully.
Do only the things you are told to do and nothing else.
If you make a mistake, cross it out. Do not use an eraser.
There are 11 parts to this activity.

The activity

1. Look at question one. Write the number 45 in the box. Now write any number in the circle to make the statement true.
2. Look at question two. Write the number 317 in the box. Now write any number in the circle to make the statement true.
3. Look at question three. Write the number 589 in the box. Now write any number in the circle to make the statement true.
4. Look at question four. Write the number 2401 in the box. Now write any number in the circle to make the statement true.
5. Look at question five. Write the number 352 in the box. Now write any two numbers in the circles to make the statement true.
6. Look at the first number line. Fill in the missing numbers.
7. Look at the second number line. Fill in the missing numbers.
8. Look at the first set of number cards. Write a number on each blank card, so that the four numbers are in order.
9. Look at the second set of number cards. Write a number on each blank card, so that the five numbers are in order.
10. Look at the numbers on the stars. Write these numbers on the triangles, in order from smallest to largest.
11. Write your name above the date.

Answers

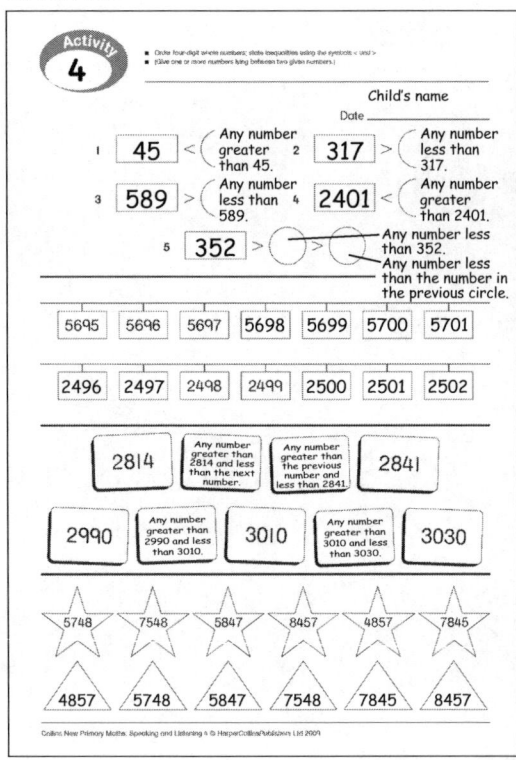

Discussion questions

- ↓ Look at the first question. What number did you write in the box/circle? (45/any number greater than 45) Read me the statement.
- ↓ Look at the first number line. Which numbers did you write down? (5698, 5699, 5700, 5701)
- ■ Look at question five. What numbers did you write in the circles? (1st circle – any number less than 352; 2nd circle – any number less than the number in the previous circle) Read me the statement.
- ■ Look at the numbers on the stars. Tell me these numbers in order, from smallest to largest. (4857, 5748, 5847, 7548, 7845, 8457)
- ↑ Come and write on the board a statement that is similar to question five. (e.g. 568 > 534 > 503; 837 < 851 < 887)
- ↑ Look at the first set of number cards. What numbers did you write on the blank number cards? (1st card – any number greater than 2814 and less than the next number; 2nd card – any number greater than the previous number and less than 2841.)

Activity 4

- Order four-digit whole numbers; state inequalities using the symbols < and >.
- (Give one or more numbers lying between two given numbers.)

Date _____

1. [ ] < ( )   2. [ ] > ( )
3. [ ] > ( )   4. [ ] < ( )
5. [ ] > ( ) > ( )

| 5695 | 5696 | 5697 | | | | |

| | | 2498 | 2499 | | | |

2814 | | | | 2841

2990 | | 3010 | | 3030

5748 | 7548 | 5847 | 8457 | 4857 | 7845

Activity 5

Year 4 Counting and understanding number

- Round (two-digit and three-digit) whole numbers.

Resources
Provide each child with the following:
- a copy of Activity 5 pupil sheet
- a pencil

Key words
zero, one, two… ten thousand   round/rounded   nearest

Say to the children:
Listen carefully.
I am going to tell you some things to do.
I will say them only once, so listen very carefully.
Do only the things you are told to do and nothing else.
If you make a mistake, cross it out. Do not use an eraser.
There are 13 parts to this activity.

The activity

1. Round 48 to the nearest 10. Write the number 48 on the racquet you rounded it to.
2. Round 93 to the nearest 10. Write the number 93 on the racquet you rounded it to.
3. Round 265 to the nearest 10. Write the number 265 on the racquet you rounded it to.
4. Round 522 to the nearest 10. Write the number 522 on the racquet you rounded it to.
5. Round 388 to the nearest 100. Write the number 388 on the racquet you rounded it to.
6. Round 534 to the nearest 100. Write the number 534 on the racquet you rounded it to.
7. Round 34 to the nearest 10. Write the number 34 on the racquet you rounded it to.
8. Round 671 to the nearest 10. Write the number 671 on the racquet you rounded it to.
9. Round 251 to the nearest 100. Write the number 251 on the racquet you rounded it to.
10. Round 75 to the nearest 10. Write the number 75 on the racquet you rounded it to.
11. Round 478 to the nearest 10. Write the number 478 on the racquet you rounded it to.
12. Round 848 to the nearest 100. Write the number 848 on the racquet you rounded it to.
13. Round 16 to the nearest 10. Write your name on that racquet.

Answers

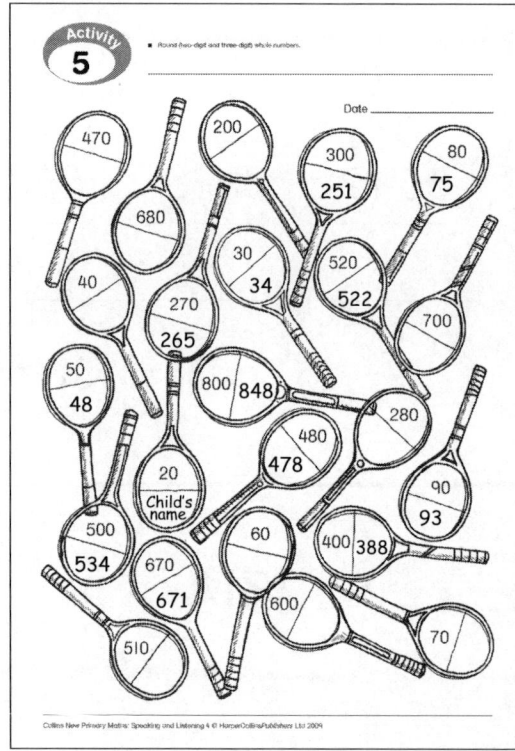

Discussion questions

↓ Choose a racquet and tell me a number you wrote on it.

↓ When do you round a three-digit number up to the next multiple of 10? (when the units digit is 5, 6, 7, 8 or 9)

■ Which number did you round to 80? (75)

■ Where did you write the number 251? (on the 300 racquet)

↑ Look at the racquets that you did not write any numbers on. Choose a racquet and tell me a number that you could write on it. (e.g. the 510 racquet could have the number 508 written on it) Why?

↑ What is 534 rounded to the nearest 100? (500)
What is 534 rounded to the nearest 10? (530)

Activity 5

■ Round (two-digit and three-digit) whole numbers.

Date _____

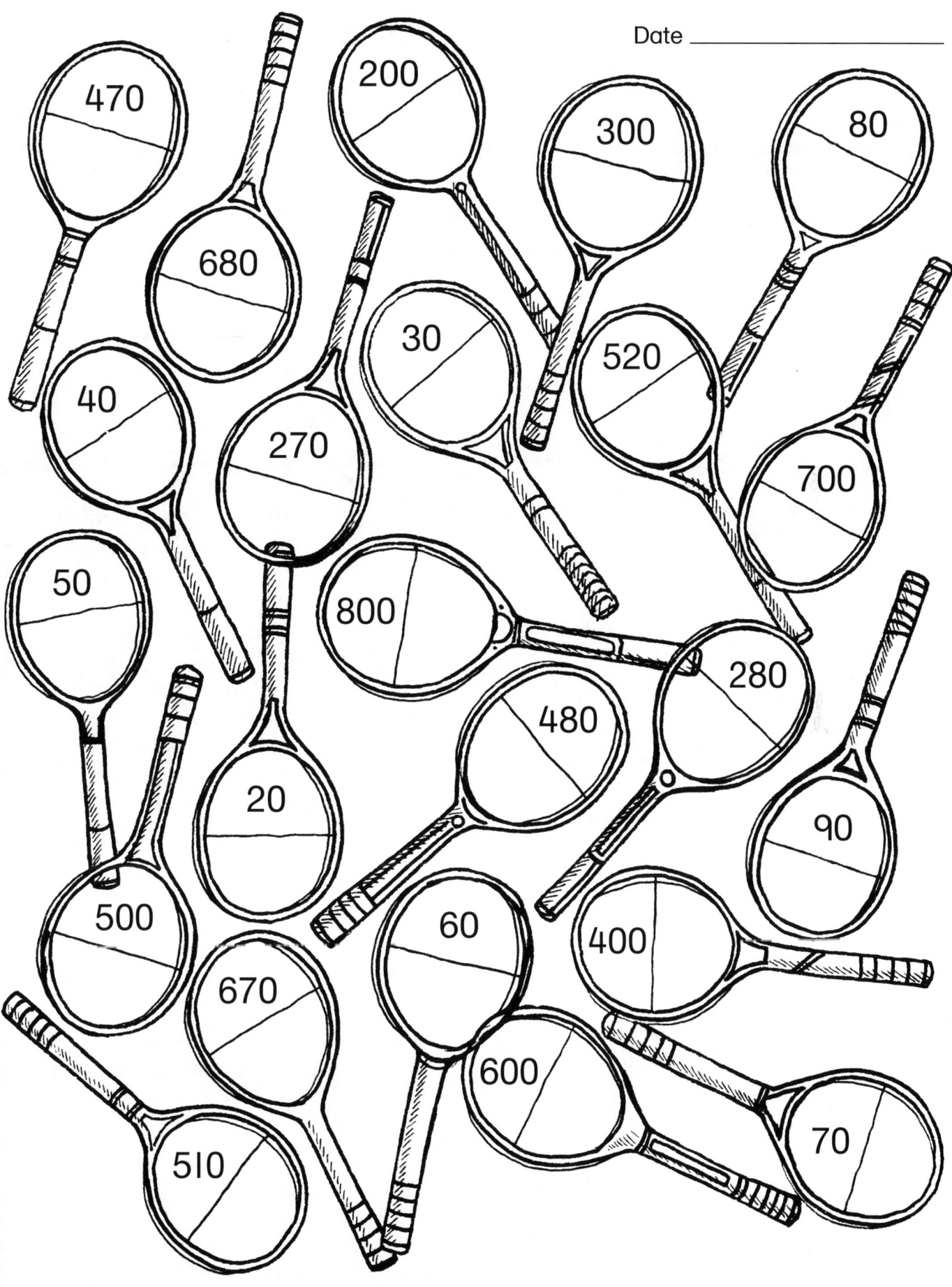

Activity 6

Year 4 Counting and understanding number

- Recognise and continue number sequences formed by counting on or back in steps of constant size (extending beyond zero when counting back).

Resources
Provide each child with the following:
- a copy of Activity 6 pupil sheet
- a red, blue, green and yellow coloured pencil

Key words
zero, one, two…one hundred   next   negative

Say to the children:
Listen carefully.
I am going to tell you some things to do.
I will say them only once, so listen very carefully.
Do only the things you are told to do and nothing else.
If you make a mistake, cross it out. Do not use an eraser.
There are 13 parts to this activity.

The activity

1. Listen carefully as I count. 83, 85, 87, 89. What number comes next? Find that number and colour the frog red.
2. 52, 48, 44, 40. What number comes next? Find that number and colour the frog red.
3. 27, 24, 21, 18. What number comes next? Find that number and colour the frog blue.
4. 26, 31, 36, 41. What number comes next? Find that number and colour the frog blue.
5. 68, 71, 74, 77. What number comes next? Find that number and colour the frog green.
6. 10, five, zero, negative five. What number comes next? Find that number and colour the frog green.
7. 21, 31, 41, 51. What number comes next? Find that number and colour the frog yellow.
8. 94, 84, 74, 64. What number comes next? Find that number and colour the frog yellow.
9. Three, seven, 11, 15. What number comes next? Find that number and colour the frog red.
10. 20, 10, zero, negative 10, negative 20. What number comes next? Find that number and colour the frog blue.
11. Five, 30, 55, 80. What number comes next? Find that number and colour the frog green.
12. Three, one, negative one, negative three. What number comes next? Find that number and colour the frog yellow.
13. Write your name under any frog you have not coloured.

Answers

Discussion questions

↓ Which numbers did you colour green? (−10, 80, 105)
↓ Give me a number sequence. What is the next number? What is the rule?
■ What number did you write your name under? Use this number in a number sequence. What is the next number? What is the rule?
■ Start at 12 and count on in fives. (17, 22, 27, 32) What do you notice? (the units digits alternate between 7 and 2) Is this always the case? (yes) How do you know? (because 7 + 5 = 12 and 12 + 5 = 17)
↑ Give me a number sequence with at least one negative number in it. What is the next number? What is the rule?
↑ Look at the numbers you did not use. Choose one of those and put it into a number sequence. What is the next number? What is the rule?

Activity 6

- Recognise and continue number sequences formed by counting on or back in steps of constant size (extending beyond zero when counting back).

Date _____

Frogs with numbers: 91, 80, 54, 0, 19, 15, −5, 55, −10, 36, 20, 61, 46, 105, −2, −30

Activity 7

Year 4 Counting and understanding number

- Identify equivalent fractions; interpret mixed numbers.

Resources
Provide each child with the following:
- a copy of Activity 7 pupil sheet
- a red, blue, green and yellow coloured pencil

Key words
one eighth, two eighths, three eighths…six eighths one half
one quarter, two quarters, three quarters three and a half
three and a quarter three and three quarters equivalent

Say to the children:
Listen carefully.
I am going to tell you some things to do.
I will say them only once, so listen very carefully.
Do only the things you are told to do and nothing else.
If you make a mistake, cross it out. Do not use an eraser.
There are 12 parts to this activity.

The activity

1. Look at the road signs. Find the road sign that is equivalent to six eighths. Colour that road sign red.
2. Find the road sign that shows three and a quarter. Colour that road sign blue.
3. Find the road sign that is equivalent to two eighths. Colour that road sign green.
4. Find the road sign that shows three and three quarters. Colour that road sign yellow.
5. Now look at the houses. Draw a chimney on one quarter of the houses.
6. Give two eighths of the houses four windows.
7. Colour five eighths of the roofs blue.
8. Give three quarters of the houses a front door.
9. Draw a small tree on the right side of one quarter of the houses.
10. Give four eighths of the houses two windows.
11. Colour three eighths of the roofs red.
12. Write your name above one eighth of the houses.

Answers

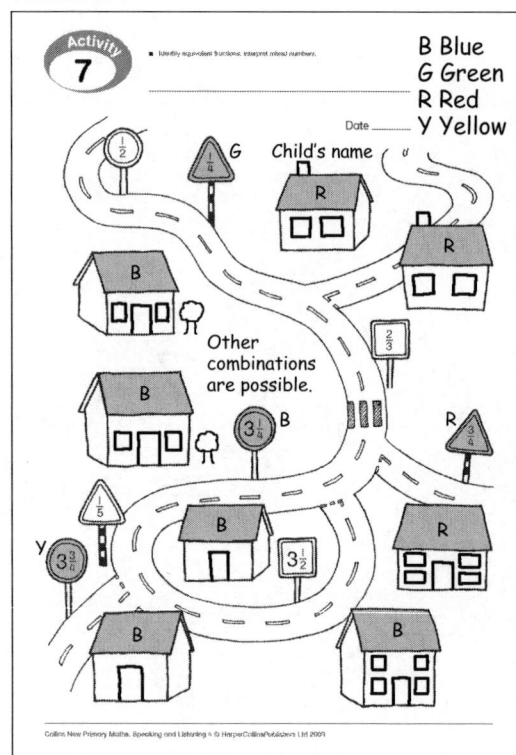

Discussion questions

↓ How many houses have a blue roof? (5)

↓ Which road sign did you colour green? ($\frac{1}{4}$)

■ What fraction of the houses have chimneys? ($\frac{1}{4}$) What is another fraction that is equivalent to one quarter? ($\frac{2}{8}, \frac{3}{12}$…)

■ What fraction of the houses have a front door? ($\frac{3}{4}$) How many is that? (6)

↑ How many houses have windows? (6) What fraction of the houses is this? ($\frac{6}{8}$ or $\frac{3}{4}$)

↑ Look at your sheet. How many houses have a red roof and a front door? (answers will vary)

Activity 7

Identify equivalent fractions; interpret mixed numbers.

Date

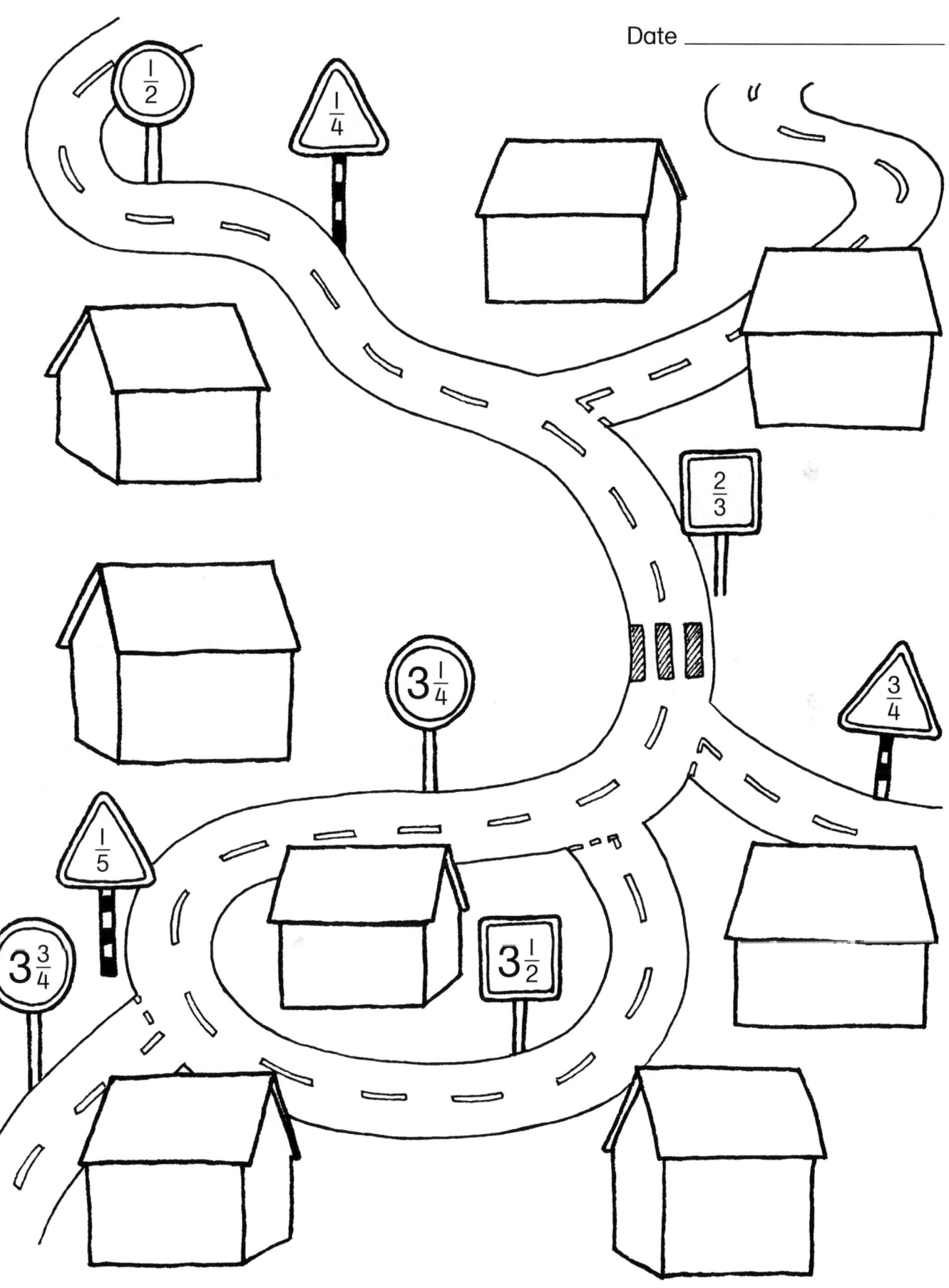

Year 4 Counting and understanding number

- Use decimal notation for tenths and hundredths and partition decimals; relate the notation to money.

Resources
Provide each child with the following:
- a copy of Activity 8 pupil sheet
- a pencil

Key words
zero, one, two…one thousand   pounds   pence   convert   round   nearest

Say to the children:
Listen carefully.
I am going to tell you some things to do.
I will say them only once, so listen very carefully.
Do only the things you are told to do and nothing else.
If you make a mistake, cross it out. Do not use an eraser.
There are 9 parts to this activity.

Answers

The activity

1. Write your name at the top of the sheet.
2. Look at the labels at the top of the sheet. The labelling machine has printed the prices in pence only. Convert each of the prices to pounds and pence and write them on the blank labels underneath.
3. Look at the loaf of bread. Round £1.53 to the nearest pound. Write the answer in the receipt under the bread.
4. Look at the carton of milk. Round 86p to the nearest pound. Write the answer in the receipt under the milk.
5. Look at the pasta. How many pence are there in £2.37? Write the answer in the receipt under the pasta.
6. Look at the box of cereal. How many pence are there in £1.14? Write the answer in the receipt under the cereal.
7. Look at the bottle of shampoo. Round £4.62 to the nearest pound. Write the answer in the receipt under the shampoo.
8. Look at the pudding. How many pence are there in £3.49? Write the answer in the receipt under the pudding.
9. Look at the bread, milk, pasta, cereal, shampoo and pudding. Sort these prices in order starting with the cheapest. Write the answers in the shopping baskets at the bottom of the sheet.

Discussion questions

↓ Look at the labels. What is 607p in pounds and pence? Can you write it on the board? (£6.07)

↓ Look at the pasta. How many pence are there in £2.37? (237p)

■ Look at the loaf of bread. What is £1.53 rounded to the nearest pound? (£2)

■ Look at the shopping baskets. Tell me the prices in order, starting with the cheapest. (86p, £1.14, £1.53, £2.37, £3.49, £4.62)

↑ How much does the loaf of bread and the packet of cereal cost altogether? (£2.67) Come and write it on the board. How many pence is that? (267p) What is that, rounded to the nearest pound? (£3)

↑ Look at the prices on the labels. Round each of these to the nearest pound. (£6, £6, £2, £11)

- Use decimal notation for tenths and hundredths and partition decimals; relate the notation to money.

Date _____

| 570p | 607p | 214p | 1106p |

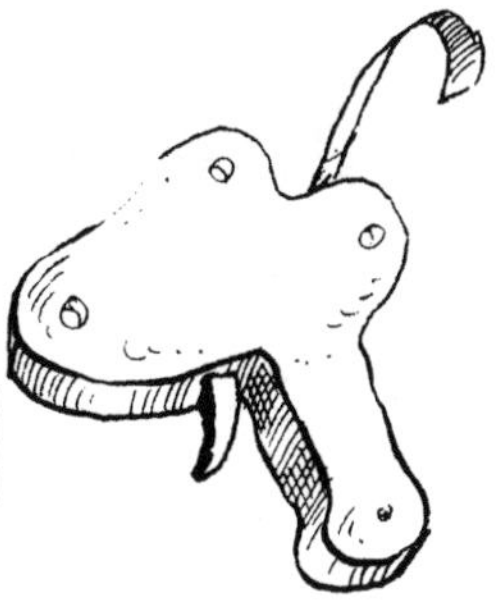

£1.53   86p   £2.37

£1.14   £4.62   £3.49

Activity 9

Year 4 Knowing and using number facts

- Use knowledge of addition and subtraction facts (to 20) and place value to derive sums and differences, (including pairs that total 100 and pairs of multiples of 50 that total 1000).

Resources
Provide each child with the following:
- a copy of Activity 9 pupil sheet
- a red, blue, green and orange coloured pencil

Key words
zero, one, two…one thousand   add   plus   more than
subtract   minus   difference between   take away   less than
first, second, third, fourth

Say to the children:
Listen carefully.
I am going to tell you some things to do.
I will say them only once, so listen very carefully.
Do only the things you are told to do and nothing else.
If you make a mistake, cross it out. Do not use an eraser.
There are 12 parts to this activity.

The activity

1. Look at the traffic lights. I am going to quickly call out five calculations. Work out the answers and colour those numbers red.
   6 add 7; 5 more than 9; 8 and 7 more; 14 add 5; 15 plus 3.

2. Look at the traffic lights again. I am going to quickly call out another five calculations. Work out the answers and colour those numbers orange.
   17 subtract 8; 12 minus 7; the difference between 19 and 3; 5 less than 16; 11 take away 4.

3. Look at the traffic lights again. I am going to quickly call out five more calculations. Work out the answers and colour those numbers green.
   13 subtract 7; 8 add 9; 5 plus 7; 20 minus 12; 15 less 13.

4. Look at the road signs. Colour red a pair of numbers that total 100.

5. Look at the road signs again. Colour blue a second pair of numbers that total 100.

6. Look at the road signs again. Colour green a third pair of numbers that total 100.

7. Again look at the road signs. Colour orange a fourth pair of numbers that total 100.

8. 64 and what other number total 100? Write your name above that road sign.

9. Look at the number plates. Colour red any pair of numbers that total 1000.

10. Look at the number plates again. Colour blue a second pair of numbers that total 1000.

11. Look at the number plates again. Colour green a third pair of numbers that total 1000.

12. Again, look at the number plates. Colour orange a fourth pair of numbers that total 1000.

Answers

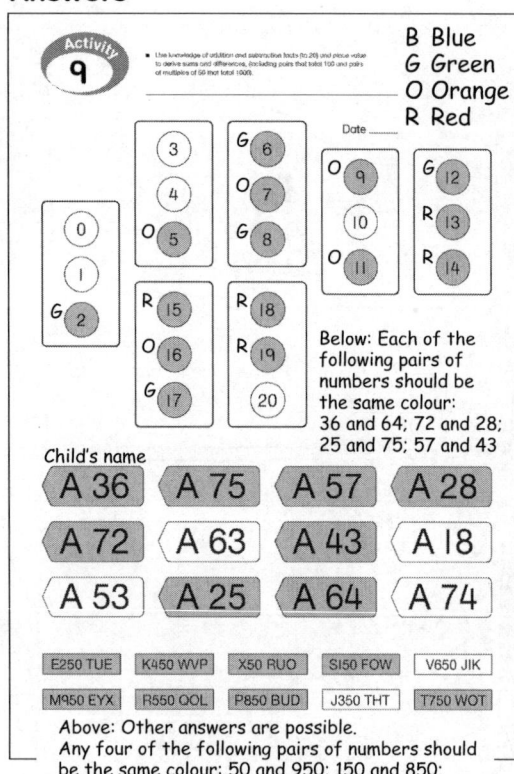

Discussion questions

- Look at your sheet. Tell me any two numbers that added together equal 100/1000? (e.g. 72 and 28/250 and 750)
- Look at the traffic lights. Choose a number you did not colour and put it into an addition/subtraction calculation.
- Look at the number plates. Which two numbers did you not colour? What do these two numbers add up to? (1000)
- Look at the traffic lights. Choose any two numbers and tell me their total/the difference between these numbers.
- Look at the road signs. Tell me a number you did not colour. (18, 53, 63, 74) What other number do you need to add to each of these numbers to make 100? (82, 47, 37, 26)
- Tell me another pair of numbers that are not on your sheet that total 100.

- Use knowledge of addition and subtraction facts (to 20) and place value to derive sums and differences, (including pairs that total 100 and pairs of multiples of 50 that total 1000).

Date _____

(0) (1) (2)

(3) (4) (5)

(6) (7) (8)

(9) (10) (11)

(12) (13) (14)

(15) (16) (17)

(18) (19) (20)

A 36   A 75   A 57   A 28

A 72   A 63   A 43   A 18

A 53   A 25   A 64   A 74

| E250 TUE | K450 WVP | X50 RUO | S150 FOW | V650 JIK |
| M950 EYX | R550 QOL | P850 BUD | J350 THT | T750 WOT |

Collins New Primary Maths: Speaking and Listening 4 © HarperCollinsPublishers Ltd 2009

Activity 10

Year 4 Knowing and using number facts

- Derive and recall multiplication facts up to 10 × 10.

Resources
Provide each child with the following:
- a copy of Activity 10 pupil sheet
- a pencil

Key words
zero, one, two…one hundred   answer   calculation   times   multiplied by   lots of   groups of   product

Say to the children:
Listen carefully.
I am going to tell you some things to do.
I will say them only once, so listen very carefully.
Do only the things you are told to do and nothing else.
If you make a mistake, cross it out. Do not use an eraser.
There are 19 parts to this activity.

The activity

1. Write your name at the top of the sheet.
2. Find calculation 5. Work out the answer and write it in the circle.
3. Now find the same number in one of the grey boxes at the side.
4. In this box there is a letter. Write this letter in boxes 8 and 20 at the bottom of the sheet.
5. Find calculation 7. Work out the answer and write it in the circle. Write the letter with the answer to calculation 7 in boxes 1 and 38.
6. Find calculation 10. Work out the answer and write it in the circle. Write the letter with the answer to calculation 10 in boxes 16, 25 and 35.
7. Find calculation 3. Work out the answer and write it in the circle. Write the letter with the answer to calculation 3 in box 36.
8. Find calculation 11. Work out the answer and write it in the circle. Write the letter with the answer to calculation 11 in box 15.
9. Find calculation 15. Work out the answer and write it in the circle. Write the letter with the answer to calculation 15 in box 44.
10. Find calculation 9. Work out the answer and write it in the circle. Write the letter with the answer to calculation 9 in boxes 4 and 40.
11. Find calculation 8. Work out the answer and write it in the circle. Write the letter with the answer to calculation 8 in boxes 13, 18, 22 and 32.
12. Find calculation 4. Work out the answer and write it in the circle. Write the letter with the answer to calculation 4 in boxes 5 and 30.
13. Find calculation 6. Work out the answer and write it in the circle. Write the letter with the answer to calculation 6 in boxes 11, 17, 19, 29 and 33.
14. Find calculation 13. Work out the answer and write it in the circle. Write the letter with the answer to calculation 13 in boxes 6, 7 and 10.
15. Find calculation 2. Work out the answer and write it in the circle. Write the letter with the answer to calculation 2 in boxes 2, 28 and 43.
16. Find calculation 12. Work out the answer and write it in the circle. Write the letter with the answer to calculation 12 in box 39.
17. Find calculation 1. Work out the answer and write it in the circle. Write the letter with the answer to calculation 1 in box 42.
18. Find calculation 16. Work out the answer and write it in the circle. Write the letter with the answer to calculation 16 in boxes 26, 27 and 31.
19. Find calculation 14. Work out the answer and write it in the circle. Write the letter with the answer to calculation 14 in box 24.

Answers

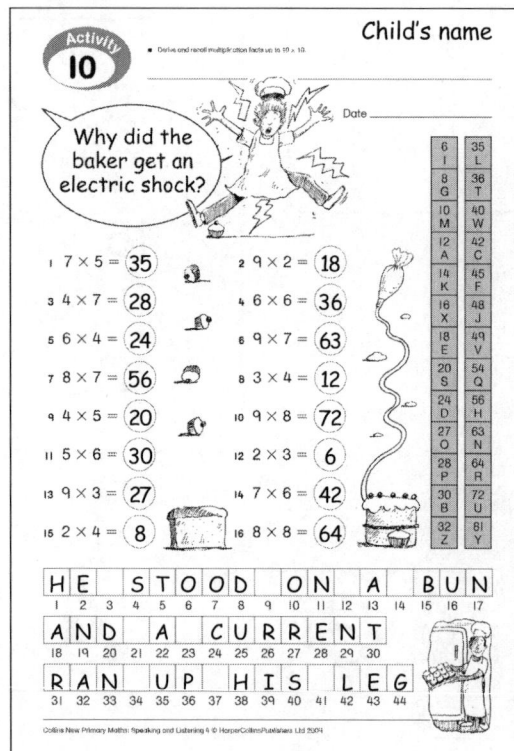

Discussion questions

↓ Why did the baker get an electric shock? (He stood on a bun and a current ran up his leg.)

↓ Tell me the answer to one of the calculations.

■ Which multiplication facts do you know by heart? Which ones do you have to think about?

■ Which calculations did you find easy/hard?

↑ What is 9 multiplied by 7? (63) What is 63 divided by 9? (7) What other multiplication and division facts do you know using the same numbers? (7 × 9 and 63 ÷ 7 = 9)

↑ Tell me a multiplication fact you know that is not on the sheet.

Activity 10

- Derive and recall multiplication facts up to 10 × 10.

Date _____

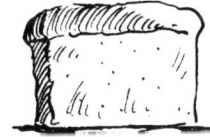

Why did the baker get an electric shock?

1. 7 × 5 =
2. 9 × 2 =
3. 4 × 7 =
4. 6 × 6 =
5. 6 × 4 =
6. 9 × 7 =
7. 8 × 7 =
8. 3 × 4 =
9. 4 × 5 =
10. 9 × 8 =
11. 5 × 6 =
12. 2 × 3 =
13. 9 × 3 =
14. 7 × 6 =
15. 2 × 4 =
16. 8 × 8 =

6 I	35 L
8 G	36 T
10 M	40 W
12 A	42 C
14 K	45 F
16 X	48 J
18 E	49 V
20 S	54 Q
24 D	56 H
27 O	63 N
28 P	64 R
30 B	72 U
32 Z	81 Y

1	2	3	4	5	6	7	8	9	10	11	12	13	14	15	16	17

18	19	20	21	22	23	24	25	26	27	28	29	30

31	32	33	34	35	36	37	38	39	40	41	42	43	44

Collins New Primary Maths: Speaking and Listening 4 © HarperCollins*Publishers* Ltd 2009

Year 4 Knowing and using number facts

- Derive and recall division facts corresponding to the 2, 3, 4, 5 and 10 times-tables.

Resources
Provide each child with the following:
- a copy of Activity 11 pupil sheet
- a red, blue, green and yellow coloured pencil

Key words
zero, one, two…one hundred   divided by   large   small

Say to the children:
Listen carefully.
I am going to tell you some things to do.
I will say them only once, so listen very carefully.
Do only the things you are told to do and nothing else.
If you make a mistake, cross it out. Do not use an eraser.
There are 17 parts to this activity.

The activity

1. What is 14 divided by two? Find that number on the large pyramid and colour it red.
2. What is 15 divided by three? Find that number on the large pyramid and colour it blue.
3. What is 30 divided by 10? Find that number on the large pyramid and colour it green.
4. What is 50 divided by five? Find that number on the small pyramid and colour it yellow.
5. What is 36 divided by four? Find that number on the large pyramid and colour it yellow.
6. What is four divided by two? Find that number on the large pyramid and colour it yellow.
7. What is 20 divided by five? Find that number on the small pyramid and colour it blue.
8. What is 24 divided by four? Find that number on the small pyramid and colour it green.
9. What is 18 divided by three? Find that number on the large pyramid and colour it green.
10. What is 20 divided by two? Find that number on the large pyramid and colour it red.
11. What is 35 divided by five? Find that number on the small pyramid and colour it red.
12. What is 12 divided by four? Find that number on the small pyramid and colour it yellow.
13. What is 90 divided by 10? Find that number on the small pyramid and colour it green.
14. What is eight divided by two? Find that number on the large pyramid and write your name in that shape.
15. What is 24 divided by three? Find that number on the small pyramid and colour it blue.
16. What is 10 divided by five? Find that number on the small pyramid and colour it red.
17. What is 32 divided by four? Find that number on the large pyramid and colour it blue.

Answers

Discussion questions

↓ Look at the small pyramid. Which numbers did you colour yellow? (3 and 10)

↓ On the large pyramid, what colour is the number six? (green)

■ What is 18 divided by three? (6)

■ Choose a number on one of the pyramids you did not colour, and put it into a division calculation.

↑ What are the two numbers you coloured green on the small pyramid? (6 and 9) What is the product of six and nine? (54) What is 54 divided by six/nine? (9/6)

↑ Using the numbers four, nine and 36, tell me two multiplication and two division calculations. (4 × 9 = 36; 9 × 4 = 36; 36 ÷ 9 = 4; 36 ÷ 4 = 9)

Activity 11

- Derive and recall division facts corresponding to the 2, 3, 4, 5 and 10 times-tables.

Date _____

Activity 12

Year 4 Knowing and using number facts

- Identify the doubles of two-digit numbers; use these to calculate doubles of multiples of 10 and 100 and derive the corresponding halves.

Resources

Provide each child with the following:
- a copy of Activity 12 pupil sheet
- a red and blue coloured pencil
- a ruler

Key words

zero, one, two…ten thousand   double   twice   multiplied by
groups of   lots of   times   product   halve/half   divided by two

Say to the children:
Listen carefully.
I am going to tell you some things to do.
I will say them only once, so listen very carefully.
Do only the things you are told to do and nothing else.
If you make a mistake, cross it out. Do not use an eraser.
There are 17 parts to this activity.

The activity

1. Put your red pencil on the dot at number 49. What is double 49? Find that number and rule a line from 49 to the dot at that number.
2. Put your red pencil on the dot at number 82. What is half of 82? Find that number and rule a line from 82 to the dot at that number.
3. Put your red pencil on the dot at number 260. What is 260 divided by two? Find that number and rule a line from 260 to the dot at that number.
4. Put your blue pencil on the dot at number 460. What is twice 460? Find that number and rule a line from 460 to the dot at that number.
5. Put your blue pencil on the dot at number 340. What is half of 340? Find that number and rule a line from 340 to the dot at that number.
6. Put your blue pencil on the dot at number 26. What is double 26? Find that number and rule a line from 26 to the dot at that number.
7. Put your blue pencil on the dot at number 6400. What is half of 6400? Find that number and rule a line from 6400 to the dot at that number.
8. Put your blue pencil on the dot at number 37. What are two lots of 37? Find that number and rule a line from 37 to the dot at that number.
9. Put your blue pencil on the dot at number 840. What is half of 840? Find that number and rule a line from 840 to the dot at that number.
10. Put your red pencil on the dot at number 3400. What is double 3400? Find that number and rule a line from 3400 to the dot at that number.
11. Put your red pencil on the dot at number 44. What is 44 divided by two? Find that number and rule a line from 44 to the dot at that number.
12. Put your blue pencil on the dot at number 96. What is half of 96? Find that number and rule a line from 96 to the dot at that number.
13. Put your blue pencil on the dot at number 330. What are two groups of 330? Find that number and rule a line from 330 to the dot at that number.
14. Put your red pencil on the dot at number 18. What is twice 18? Find that number and rule a line from 18 to the dot at that number.
15. Put your red pencil on the dot at number 4800. What is 4800 divided by two? Find that number and rule a line from 4800 to the dot at that number.
16. Put your red pencil on the dot at number 4700. What is double 4700? Find that number and rule a line from 4700 to the dot at that number.
17. Write your name under the date.

Answers

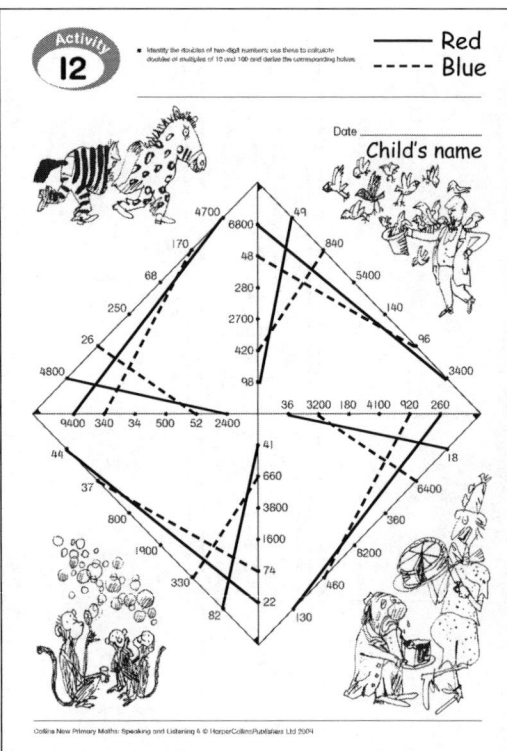

Discussion questions

- ↓ What is double 18? (36) What is half of 18? (9)
- ↓ What is half of 360? (180)
- Did you find this activity easy or difficult? Why?
- Choose two numbers and tell me two facts about them. (eg. 180 × 2 = 360; 360 ÷ 2 = 180)
- ↑ What is the relationship between the numbers 140 and 280?
- ↑ Tell me a number that is not on the sheet and double/halve it.

Activity 12

- Identify the doubles of two-digit numbers; use these to calculate doubles of multiples of 10 and 100 and derive the corresponding halves.

Date _____

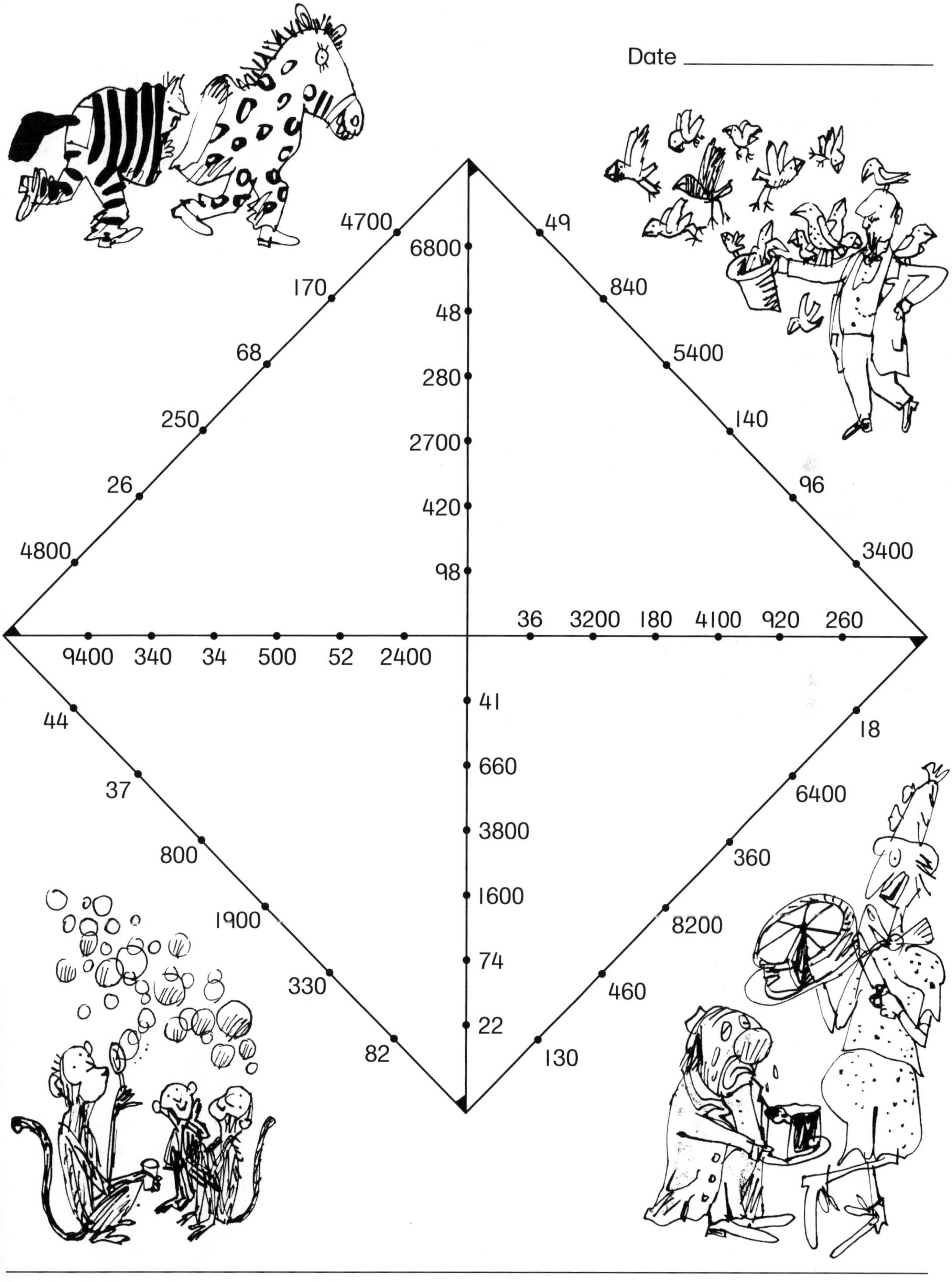

4700
6800
170
49
48
840
68
280
5400
250
140
2700
26
96
420
4800
98
3400
36 3200 180 4100 920 260
9400 340 34 500 52 2400
41
44
660
18
37
3800
6400
800
360
1600
1900
8200
74
330
460
22
82
130

Activity 13

Year 4 Calculating

- Add or subtract mentally pairs of two-digit whole numbers.

Resources
Provide each child with the following:
- a copy of Activity 13 pupil sheet
- a pencil

Key words
zero, one, two…ten thousand   add   total   more than   plus   subtract   minus   take away   difference   less

Say to the children:
Listen carefully.
I am going to tell you some things to do.
I will say them only once, so listen very carefully.
Do only the things you are told to do and nothing else.
If you make a mistake, cross it out. Do not use an eraser.
There are 10 parts to this activity.

The activity

Look at the sheet. It shows a football pitch. This activity is like playing a game of football, but some of the rules are different. In our game there are 18 players a side and there are lots of goalkeepers. Circles are Wellton Town and squares are Torcross United. When a ball is passed from one player to another you draw a straight line. If the ball goes to a number in a circle in the shaded part of Wellton Town's net, it is a goal for Wellton Town. If the ball goes to a number in a square in the shaded part of Torcross United's net, it is a goal for Torcross United. Each goal scores one point.

1. Place your pencil on the dot at the word Start.
2. The ball passes to the answer to 328 plus 40.
3. He passes to the difference between 37 and 100, who passes to the total of 829 add three, who passes to 400 add 800.
4. He then passes the ball to the difference between 4700 and 5000, who passes to the difference between 74 and 100, who passes to 203 subtract nine, who passes to 1500 minus 600.
5. He then passes the ball to 52 less 34, who passes to the difference between 7200 and 8000, who passes to 46 plus 300, who passes to 30 more than 80.
6. He then passes the ball to 634 plus 50, who passes to 400 add 371, who passes to 34 plus 28, who passes to 4372 add six, who passes to 684 minus 30.
7. He then passes the ball to 504 take away seven, who passes to 200 more than 684, who passes to 4000 add 518, who passes to 160 subtract 70.
8. He then passes to 97 plus 700, who passes to 2000 add 263, who passes to 82 minus 67, who passes to 1200 less 500.
9. The whistle blows. Put each team's score in the box at the bottom of the sheet.
10. Write your name under the word Start.

Answers

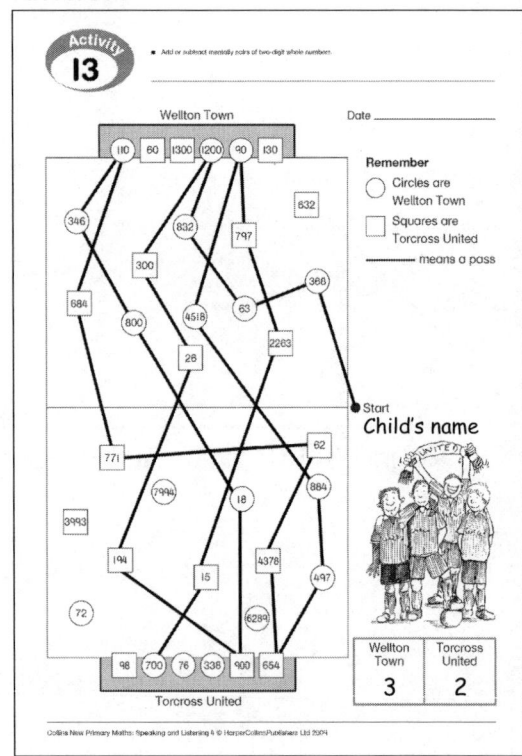

Discussion questions

↓ Who won the game? (Wellton Town)

↓ What is 46 add 30? (76) How did you work it out? Did anyone work it out a different way?

■ Why didn't Torcross United score three goals? (the last pass was 82 – 67 which equals 15, who passed to 1200 – 500, which is 700, but 700 is in the opposing team)

■ Choose a number from the Wellton Town team that did not handle the ball during the game. What two other numbers will total that number? (e.g. 338: 378 – 40)

↑ What is 4000 subtract seven? (3993) How did you work it out? Did anyone work it out using another method? Which team is this player on? (Torcross United)

↑ Did you find this activity easy or hard? Why?

Activity 13

- Add or subtract mentally pairs of two-digit whole numbers.

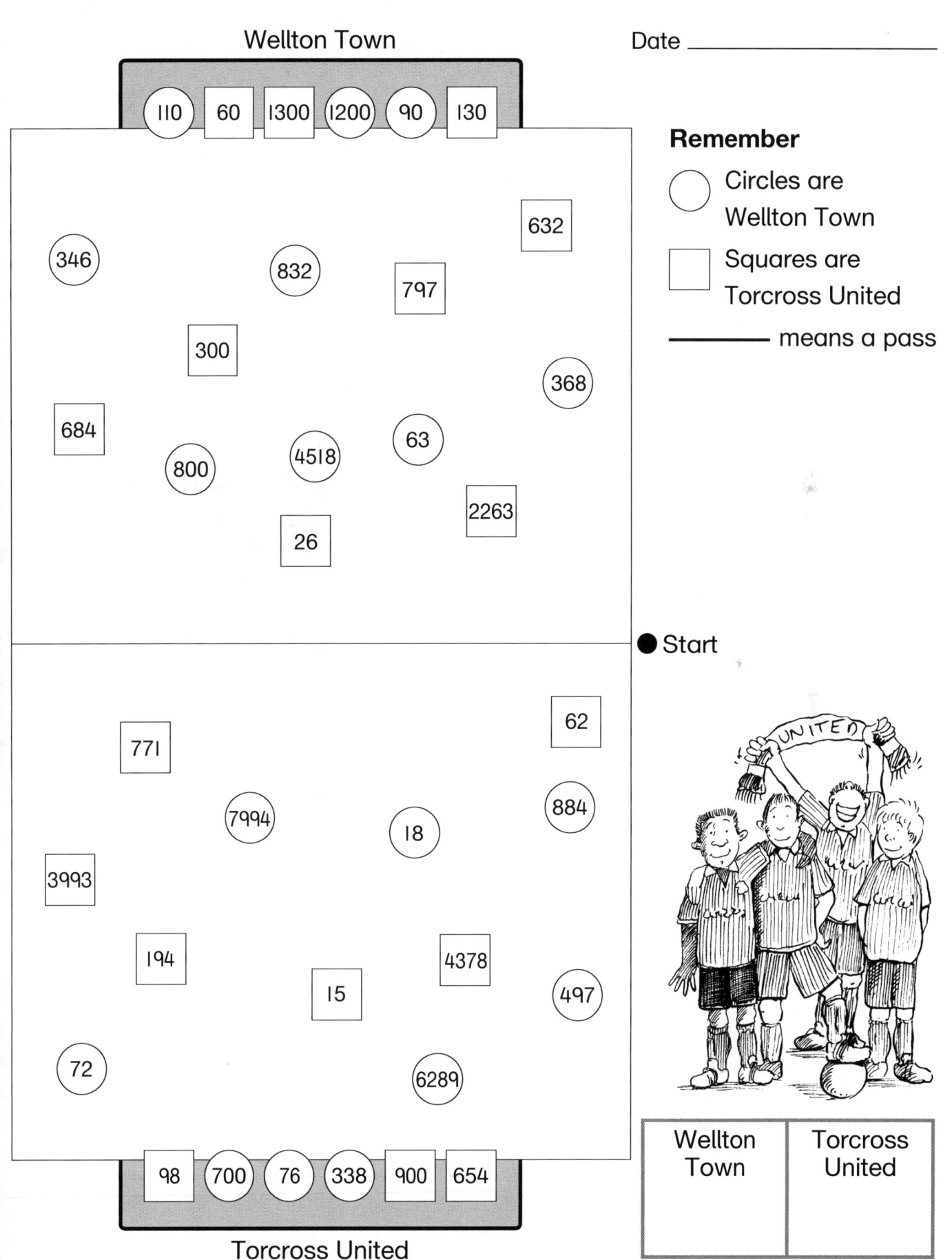

Date _____

Wellton Town

110, 60, 1300, 1200, 90, 130

346, 832, 632, 797, 300, 368, 684, 63, 800, 4518, 2263, 26

Start

771, 62, 7994, 884, 18, 3993, 194, 4378, 15, 497, 72, 6289

98, 700, 76, 338, 900, 654

Torcross United

Remember

◯ Circles are Wellton Town

☐ Squares are Torcross United

—— means a pass

Wellton Town	Torcross United

Collins New Primary Maths: Speaking and Listening 4 © HarperCollins*Publishers* Ltd 2009

Activity 14

Year 4 Calculating

- Refine and use efficient written methods to add two-digit and three-digit whole numbers (and more than two whole numbers).

Resources
Provide each child with the following:
- a copy of Activity 14 pupil sheet
- a red, blue, green and yellow coloured pencil
- a pencil

Key words
zero, one, two…two thousand   number   smallest   add   sum   total

Say to the children:
Listen carefully.
I am going to tell you some things to do.
I will say them only once, so listen very carefully.
Do only the things you are told to do and nothing else.
If you make a mistake, cross it out. Do not use an eraser.
There are 7 parts to this activity.

The activity

1. Look at the numbers on the board. Colour red the numbers 57, 38 and 76. Add these three numbers together and write the answer in box one.

2. Colour blue the numbers 432, 79 and 8. Add these three numbers together and write the answer in box two.

3. Colour green the numbers 256, 83 and 54. Find the sum of these three numbers and write the answer in box three.

4. Colour yellow the numbers 42, 85, 37 and 19. Add these four numbers together and write the answer in box four.

5. Look at the remaining numbers on the board. Find the total of these numbers and write the answer in box five.

6. Look at the numbers you have written in boxes one, two and three. Add these three numbers together and write the answer in box six.

7. Look at the six answers you have just written down. Write your name below the smallest number.

Answers

B Blue
G Green
R Red
Y Yellow

Board numbers:
R 57, B 11, B 79, G 83
Y 19, G 54, B 432, R 38
Y 85, R 76, G 256
Y 37, Y 81, Y 42
B 8, 29, 304

1. 171
2. 519
3. 393
4. 183
5. 425
6. 1083

Discussion questions

↓ What number did you write in box three? (393)

↓ Look at your working out. Choose a calculation and tell me how you worked it out.

■ Look at all the numbers you coloured red. What is the total of these three numbers? (171)

■ Look at the number you have written in boxes one, two and three. What is the total of these three numbers? (1083) Where did you write the answer? (in box six)

↑ Choose any three/four/five numbers from the board and add them together.

↑ Look at the number you have written in boxes one, two, three, four and five. What is the total of these five numbers? (1691)

Activity 14

- Refine and use efficient written methods to add two-digit and three-digit whole numbers (and more than two whole numbers).

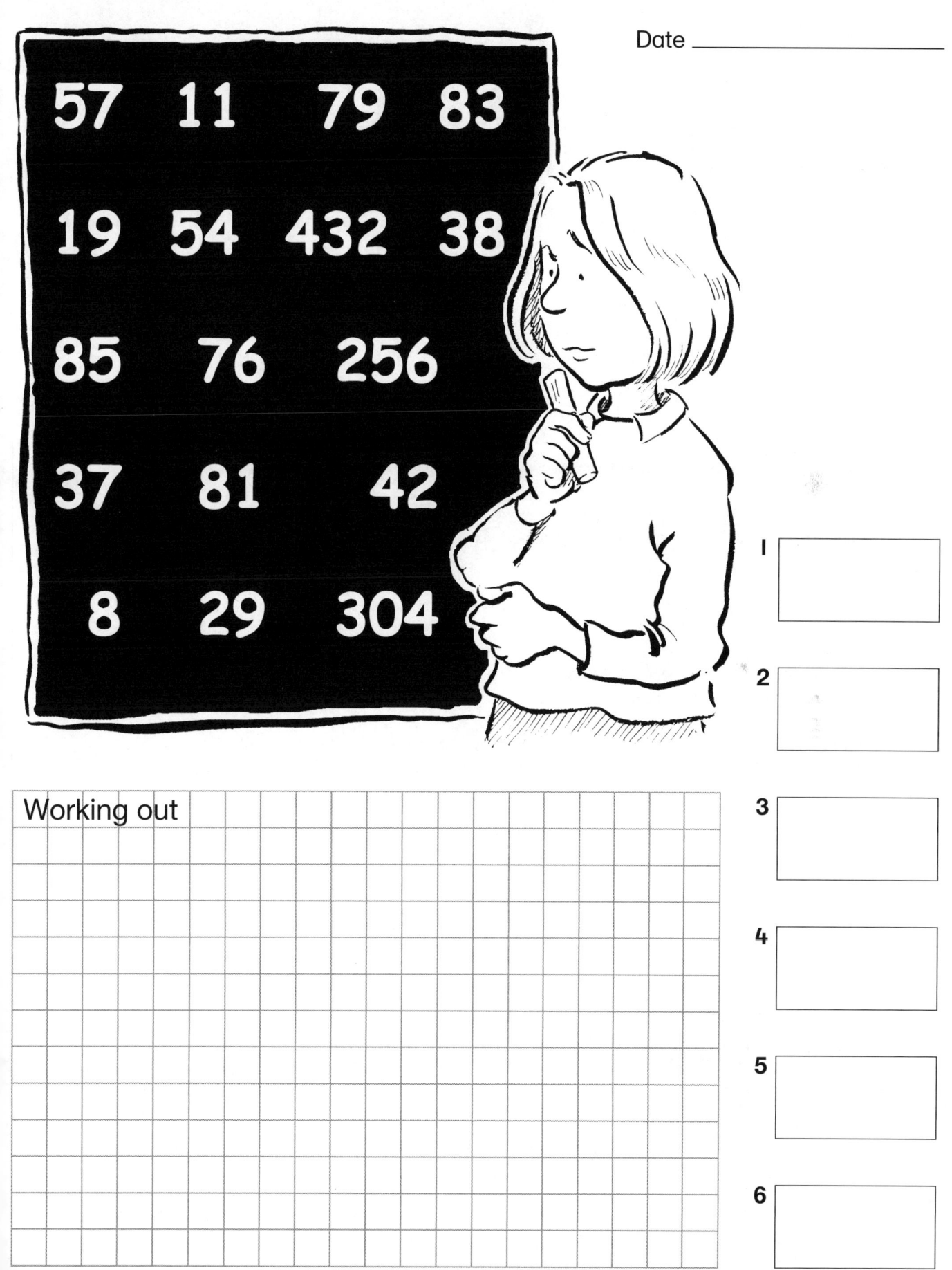

Date _____

57	11	79	83
19	54	432	38
85	76	256	
37	81	42	
8	29	304	

1.
2.
3.
4.
5.
6.

Working out

Activity 15

Year 4 Calculating

- Refine and use efficient written methods to add and subtract two-digit and three-digit whole numbers.

Resources
Provide each child with the following:
- a copy of Activity 15 pupil sheet
- a pencil

Key words
zero, one, two…two thousand   number   smallest   largest   first   last   reversing   digits   add   subtract   take away   difference

Say to the children:
Listen carefully.
I am going to tell you some things to do.
I will say them only once, so listen very carefully.
Do only the things you are told to do and nothing else.
If you make a mistake, cross it out. Do not use an eraser.
There are 7 parts to this activity.

The activity

1. Look at row a. Add the smallest number to the largest number. Write the answer in box one.

2. Look at row a again. Subtract the first number from the last number. Write the answer in box two.

3. Look at row b. Add the largest number to itself. Write the answer in box three.

4. Look at row b again. Find the difference between the smallest number and the largest number. Write the answer in box four.

5. Look at row c. Find the largest number. Write a new number by reversing its digits. Now add these two numbers together. Write the answer in box five.

6. Look at row c again. Take the smallest number away from the largest number. Write the answer in box six.

7. Look at the six answers you have just written down. Write your name under the largest number.

Answers

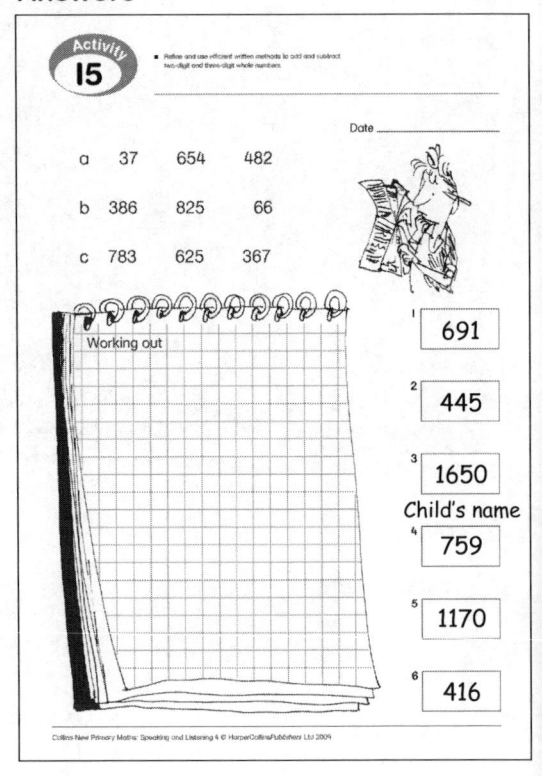

a	37	654	482
b	386	825	66
c	783	625	367

1. 691
2. 445
3. 1650
4. 759
5. 1170
6. 416

Discussion questions

- ↓ What number did you write in box one? (691)

- ↓ Look at your working out. Choose a calculation and explain to me how you worked it out.

- ■ Look at row b. You were asked to add the largest number to itself. What is the answer? (1650) How did you work it out? Did anyone work it out using a different method? What is the quickest way?

- ■ Look at row c. What is the largest number? (783) What new number can you make by reversing its digits? (387) What is the sum of these two numbers? (1170)

- ↑ What numbers did you write in boxes four and six? (759 and 416) What is the total of these two numbers? (1175) What is the difference between these two numbers? (343)

- ↑ Look at all the numbers in rows a, b and c. Choose any two numbers and add them together. What is the difference between the two numbers?

Activity 15

- Refine and use efficient written methods to add and subtract two-digit and three-digit whole numbers.

Date _____

a   37   654   482

b   386   825   66

c   783   625   367

Working out

1
2
3
4
5
6

Collins New Primary Maths: Speaking and Listening 4 © HarperCollinsPublishers Ltd 2009

Activity 16

Year 4 Calculating

- Refine and use efficient written methods to add and subtract two-digit and three-digit whole numbers and £.p.

Resources
Provide each child with the following:
- a copy of Activity 16 pupil sheet
- a pencil

Key words
zero, one, two…one hundred   pounds   pence   price   cost   cheapest   expensive   total   subtract   take away   difference   altogether

Say to the children:
Listen carefully.
I am going to tell you some things to do.
I will say them only once, so listen very carefully.
Do only the things you are told to do and nothing else.
If you make a mistake, cross it out. Do not use an eraser.
There are 7 parts to this activity.

The activity

1. What is the total cost of the books and the racquet? Write the answer in box one.

2. How much does the board game and the cup and saucer cost altogether? Write the answer in box two.

3. What is the difference in price between the teddy bear and the kettle? Write the answer in box three.

4. What is the difference in price between the board game and the racquet? Write the answer in box four.

5. What is the total cost of the cup and saucer and the teddy bear? Write the answer in box five.

6. What is the difference in price between the cheapest and the most expensive item on the stall? Write the answer in box six.

7. If you were to buy one of the items from the jumble sale with a five pound note you would receive 24p change. Write your name under that item.

Answers

1. £9.42
2. £8.63
3. £2.12
4. £2.61
5. £9.99
6. £4.41

Discussion questions

↓ What number did you write in box four? (£2.61)

↓ Look at your working out. Choose a calculation and tell me how you worked it out.

■ What is the total cost of the cup and saucer and the teddy bear? (£9.99)
Where did you write that total? (in box five)

■ What answer did you write in box two? (£8.63) Round this to the nearest pound. (£9)

↑ Look at all the items on the table. Choose any two items and work out their total cost. What is their difference in price?

↑ Look at all the items on the table. Choose any three items and work out how much they cost altogether.

Activity 16

- Refine and use efficient written methods to add and subtract two-digit and three-digit whole numbers and £.p.

Date _____

Jumble Sale

- £6·48
- £3·87
- £2·94
- £4·76
- £5·23
- £7·35

Working out

1.
2.
3.
4.
5.
6.

Collins New Primary Maths: Speaking and Listening 4 © HarperCollinsPublishers Ltd 2009

Activity 17

Year 4 Calculating

- Multiply and divide numbers to 1000 by 10 and then 100 (whole-number answers), understanding the effect; relate to scaling up or down.
- (Add and subtract 1, 10, 100 and 1000 to or from any whole number.)

Resources
Provide each child with the following:
- a copy of Activity 17 pupil sheet
- a red, blue, green and yellow coloured pencil

Key words
zero, one, two…ten thousand   more   less   tens   hundreds   thousands   multiply by   times   divided by

Say to the children:
Listen carefully.
I am going to tell you some things to do.
I will say them only once, so listen very carefully.
Do only the things you are told to do and nothing else.
If you make a mistake, cross it out. Do not use an eraser.
There are 17 parts to this activity.

The activity

1. Listen carefully as I count. 743, 843, 943, 1043. What number comes next? Find that number and colour it red.
2. 5315, 6315, 7315, 8315. What number comes next? Find that number and colour it blue.
3. 4231, 4221, 4211, 4201. What number comes next? Find that number and colour it green.
4. What is one more than 7243? Find that number and colour it yellow.
5. What is one less than 6220? Find that number and colour it red.
6. What is 10 more than 4874? Find that number and colour it blue.
7. What is 1000 more than 2360? Find that number and colour it green.
8. What is 1000 less than 8023? Find that number and colour it yellow.
9. What is 100 less than 5062? Find that number and colour it red.
10. What is 27 multiplied by 10? Find that number and colour it blue.
11. What is 60 divided by 10? Find that number and colour it green.
12. What is 41 times 1000? Find that number and colour it yellow
13. What is 8000 divided by 10? Find that number and colour it red.
14. What is 342 multiplied by 10? Find that number and colour it blue.
15. What is 72 times 100? Find that number and colour it green.
16. What is 200 divided by 10? Find that number and colour it yellow.
17. Write your name on the astronaut's helmet.

Answers

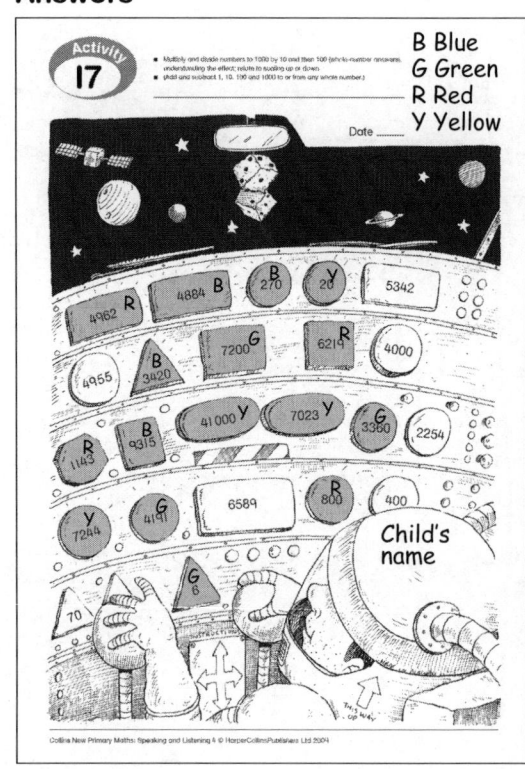

B Blue
G Green
R Red
Y Yellow

Discussion questions

↓ What colour is the number 3360? (green)

↓ Which numbers did you colour red? (800, 1143, 4962, 6219)

■ What is one more/10 more/100 more/1000 more than 4884? (4885, 4894, 4984, 5884)

■ What is one less/10 less/100 less/1000 less than 6219? (6218, 6209, 6119, 5219)

↑ What is 34 multiplied by 10/multiplied by 100? (340/3400)

↑ What is 6000 divided by 10/divided by 100/divided by 1000? (600/60/6)

Activity 17

- Multiply and divide numbers to 1000 by 10 and then 100 (whole-number answers), understanding the effect; relate to scaling up or down.
- (Add and subtract 1, 10, 100 and 1000 to or from any whole number.)

Date _____

Numbers on the control panel:

4962, 4884, 270, 20, 5342, 4955, 3420, 7200, 6219, 4000, 1143, 9315, 41 000, 7023, 3360, 2254, 7244, 4191, 6589, 800, 400, 70, 6

INSTRUCTIONS

THIS WAY UP

Activity 18

Year 4 Calculating

- Multiply and divide numbers to 1000 by 10 and then 100 (whole-number answers), understanding the effect; relate to scaling up or down.
- Derive and recall multiplication facts up to 10 × 10, the corresponding division facts and multiples of numbers to 10 up to the tenth multiple.

Resources
Provide each child with the following:
- a copy of Activity 18 pupil sheet
- a red, blue, green and yellow coloured pencil

Key words
zero, one, two…ten thousand   multiplied by   times
lots of   groups of   twice   double   divided by   one tenth
one hundredth   half

Say to the children:
Listen carefully.
I am going to tell you some things to do.
I will say them only once, so listen very carefully.
Do only the things you are told to do and nothing else.
If you make a mistake, cross it out. Do not use an eraser.
There are 21 parts to this activity.

The activity

1. What is 427 multiplied by 10? Find that number and colour that shape red.
2. What is 7000 divided by 100? Find that number and colour that shape green.
3. What is 65 times two? Find that number and colour that shape yellow.
4. What is 160 divided by two? Find that number and colour that shape blue.
5. What are four groups of 30? Find that number and colour that shape green.
6. What is 56 multiplied by 100? Find that number and colour that shape green.
7. What is the product of 16 and four? Find that number and colour that shape blue.
8. What is one tenth of 3000? Find that number and colour that shape red.
9. What is 150 divided by two? Find that number and colour that shape green.
10. What is twice 95? Find that number and colour that shape blue.
11. What is half of 130? Find that number and colour that shape green.
12. What is one hundredth of 600? Find that number and colour that shape blue.
13. What is 70 multiplied by six? Find that number and colour that shape red.
14. What are three lots of 18? Find that number and colour that shape red.
15. What is ten times 84? Find that number and colour that shape green.
16. What is one hundredth of 1000? Find that number and colour that shape green.
17. What is 80 times seven? Find that number and colour that shape yellow.
18. What is one tenth of 200? Find that number and colour that shape blue.
19. What is 34 multiplied by five? Find that number and colour that shape green.
20. What is 200 divided by two? Find that number and colour that shape red.
21. Turn the sheet upside down and write your name on the bottom step.

Answers

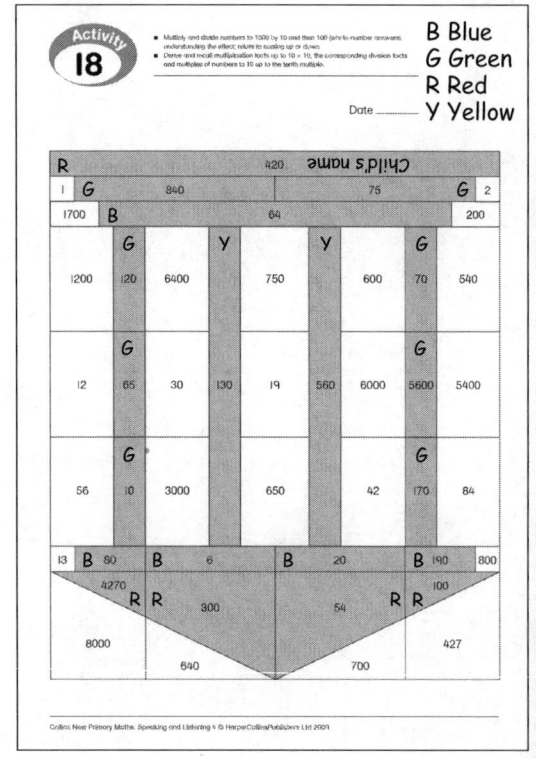

B Blue
G Green
R Red
Y Yellow

Discussion questions

↓ What have you coloured? (a Greek temple)

↓ What is 65 times two? (130) What colour is the shape with 130 in it? (yellow)

■ What is one hundredth of 7000? (70) What is one tenth of 7000? (700)

■ What numbers did you colour yellow? (130/560)

↑ If 18 multiplied by three equals 54, what is 54 divided by three? (18) Why?

↑ Choose a number you did not colour and put it into a multiplication and division calculation.

Activity 18

- Multiply and divide numbers to 1000 by 10 and then 100 (whole-number answers), understanding the effect; relate to scaling up or down.
- Derive and recall multiplication facts up to 10 × 10, the corresponding division facts and multiples of numbers to 10 up to the tenth multiple.

Date _____

		420			
1	840		75		2
1700		64			200

1200	120	6400	750	600	70	540
12	65	30	130	19	560	6000	5600	5400
56	10	3000		650		42	170	84

13	80	6	20	190	800
	4270	300	54	100	
	8000	640	700	427	

Collins New Primary Maths: Speaking and Listening 4 © HarperCollins*Publishers* Ltd 2009

Activity 19

Year 4 Calculating

- Develop and use written methods to record, support and explain multiplication of two-digit numbers by a one-digit number.

Resources

Provide each child with the following:
- a copy of Activity 19 pupil sheet
- a pencil

You will also need a 0 – 9 die

Key words

zero, one, two…one thousand answer calculation times multiplied by lots of groups of product

Say to the children:

Listen carefully.

I am going to tell you some things to do.

I will say them only once, so listen very carefully.

Do only the things you are told to do and nothing else.

If you make a mistake, cross it out. Do not use an eraser.

There are 7 parts to this activity.

The activity

Note: Italicised instructions are for the teacher and are not to be read out to the children.

1. (*Roll the die and call out the number rolled.*) Write the number (*die number rolled*) in the circle in question one. Work out the answer and write it in the box in question one.

2. (*Roll the die and call out the number rolled.*) Write the number (*die number rolled*) in the circle in question two. Work out the answer and write it in the box in question two.

3. (*Roll the die and call out the number rolled.*) Write the number (*die number rolled*) in the circle in question three. Work out the answer and write it in the box in question three.

4. (*Roll the die and call out the number rolled.*) Write the number (*die number rolled*) in the circle in question four. Work out the answer and write it in the box in question four.

5. (*Roll the die and call out the number rolled.*) Write the number (*die number rolled*) in the circle in question five. Work out the answer and write it in the box in question five.

6. (*Roll the die and call out the number rolled.*) Write the number (*die number rolled*) in the circle in question six. Work out the answer and write it in the box in question six.

7. Look at all the answers in the boxes. Write your name under the largest number.

Answers

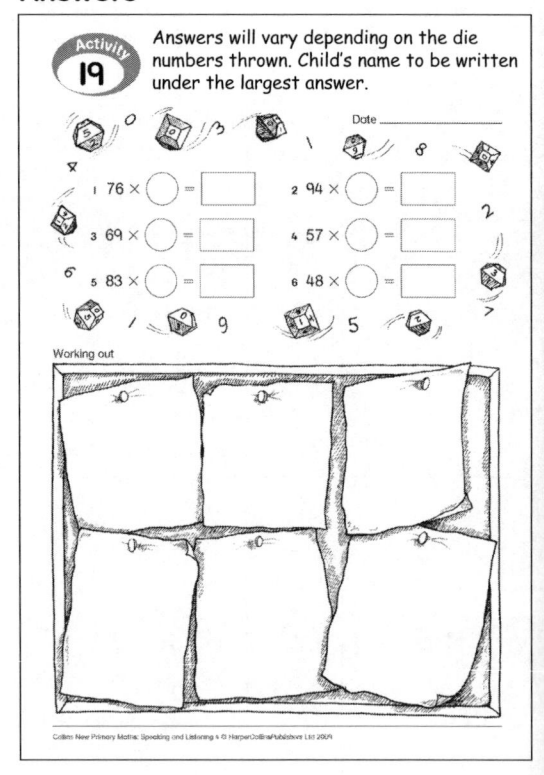

Answers will vary depending on the die numbers thrown. Child's name to be written under the largest answer.

Discussion questions

↓ What is the answer to question one?

↓ Choose a calculation, tell me the answer and explain how you worked it out.

■ What is the answer to question four? How did you work it out? Did anyone work it out using a different method?

■ Which calculations did you find easy/hard? Why?

↑ Did you work out the answers to any of these calculations in your head? Which ones? How did you work it out?

↑ Did you answer any calculations incorrectly? Which ones? What is the correct answer? Do you know why you got an incorrect answer?

Activity 19

- Develop and use written methods to record, support and explain multiplication of two-digit numbers by a one-digit number.

Date _____

1. 76 × ◯ = ☐
2. 94 × ◯ = ☐
3. 69 × ◯ = ☐
4. 57 × ◯ = ☐
5. 83 × ◯ = ☐
6. 48 × ◯ = ☐

Working out

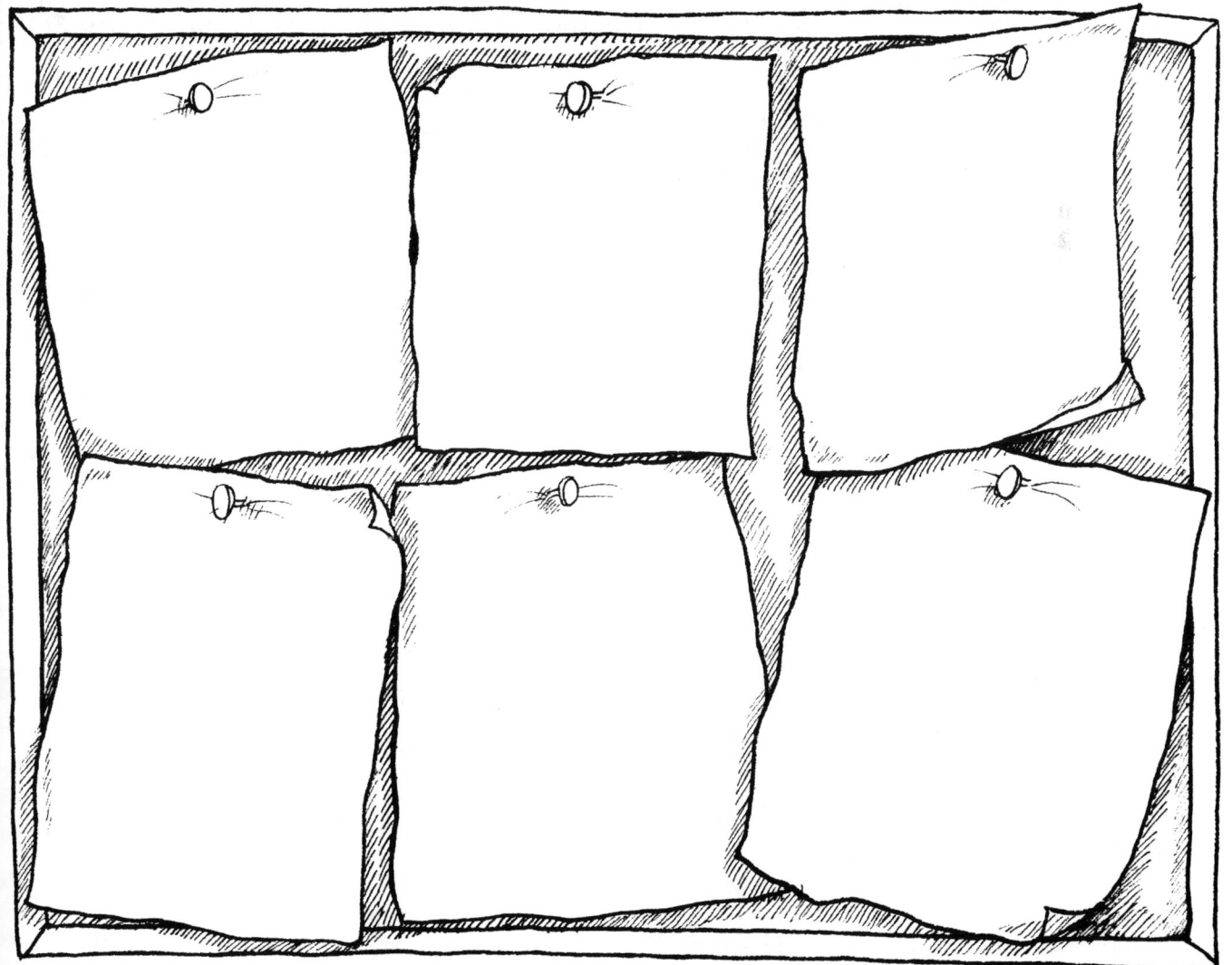

Activity 20

Year 4 Calculating

- Develop and use written methods to record, support and explain division of two-digit numbers by a one-digit number, including division with remainders.

Resources
Provide each child with the following:
- a copy of Activity 20 pupil sheet
- a pencil

Key words
zero, one, two…one hundred   divided by   divided into

Say to the children:
Listen carefully.
I am going to tell you some things to do.
I will say them only once, so listen very carefully.
Do only the things you are told to do and nothing else.
If you make a mistake, cross it out. Do not use an eraser.
There are 14 parts to this activity.

The activity

1. Draw a ring around number 10. This is your start number.
2. What is 10 divided by four? What is the remainder? Count on that number from 10 and draw a ring around the number you reach. This is your new start number.
3. Look at your new start number. What does five divided into this number equal? What is the remainder? Count on that number and draw a ring around the number you reach. This is your new start number.
4. Look at your new start number. What does five divided into this number equal? What is the remainder? Count on that number and draw a ring around the number you reach. This is your new start number.
5. Look at your new start number. What does four divided into this number equal? What is the remainder? Count on that number and draw a ring around the number you reach. This is your new start number.
6. Look at your new start number. What does three divided into this number equal? What is the remainder? Count on that number and draw a ring around the number you reach. This is your new start number.
7. Look at your new start number. What does three divided into this number equal? What is the remainder? Count on that number and draw a ring around the number you reach. This is your new start number.
8. Look at your new start number. What does 10 divided into this number equal? What is the remainder? Count on that number and draw a ring around the number you reach. This is your new start number.
9. Look at your new start number. What does five divided into this number equal? What is the remainder? Count on that number and draw a ring around the number you reach. This is your new start number.
10. Look at your new start number. What does four divided into this number equal? What is the remainder? Count on that number and draw a ring around the number you reach. This is your new start number.
11. Look at your new start number. What does four divided into this number equal? What is the remainder? Count on that number and draw a ring around the number you reach. This is your new start number.
12. Look at your new start number. What does 10 divided into this number equal? What is the remainder? Count on that number and draw a ring around the number you reach. This is your new start number.
13. Look at your new start number. What does five divided into this number equal? What is the remainder? Count on that number and draw a cross through this number.
14. Write your name in the pool at the bottom of the sheet.

Answers

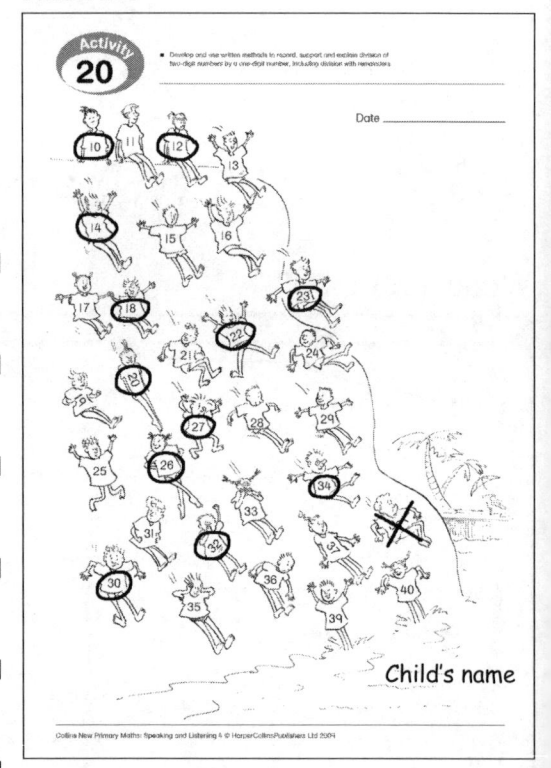

Discussion questions

↓ What was the final number? (38)

↓ Did you find this activity easy or hard? Why?

■ What is 18 divided by five? (3 r 3)

■ Call out the numbers you drew a circle around. (10, 12, 14, 18, 20, 22, 23, 26, 27, 30, 32 and 34)

↑ Choose one of the numbers you did not draw a ring around and put it into a division calculation.

↑ Which division facts do you find easy to answer? Why are these facts easy?

Activity 20

- Develop and use written methods to record, support and explain division of two-digit numbers by a one-digit number, including division with remainders.

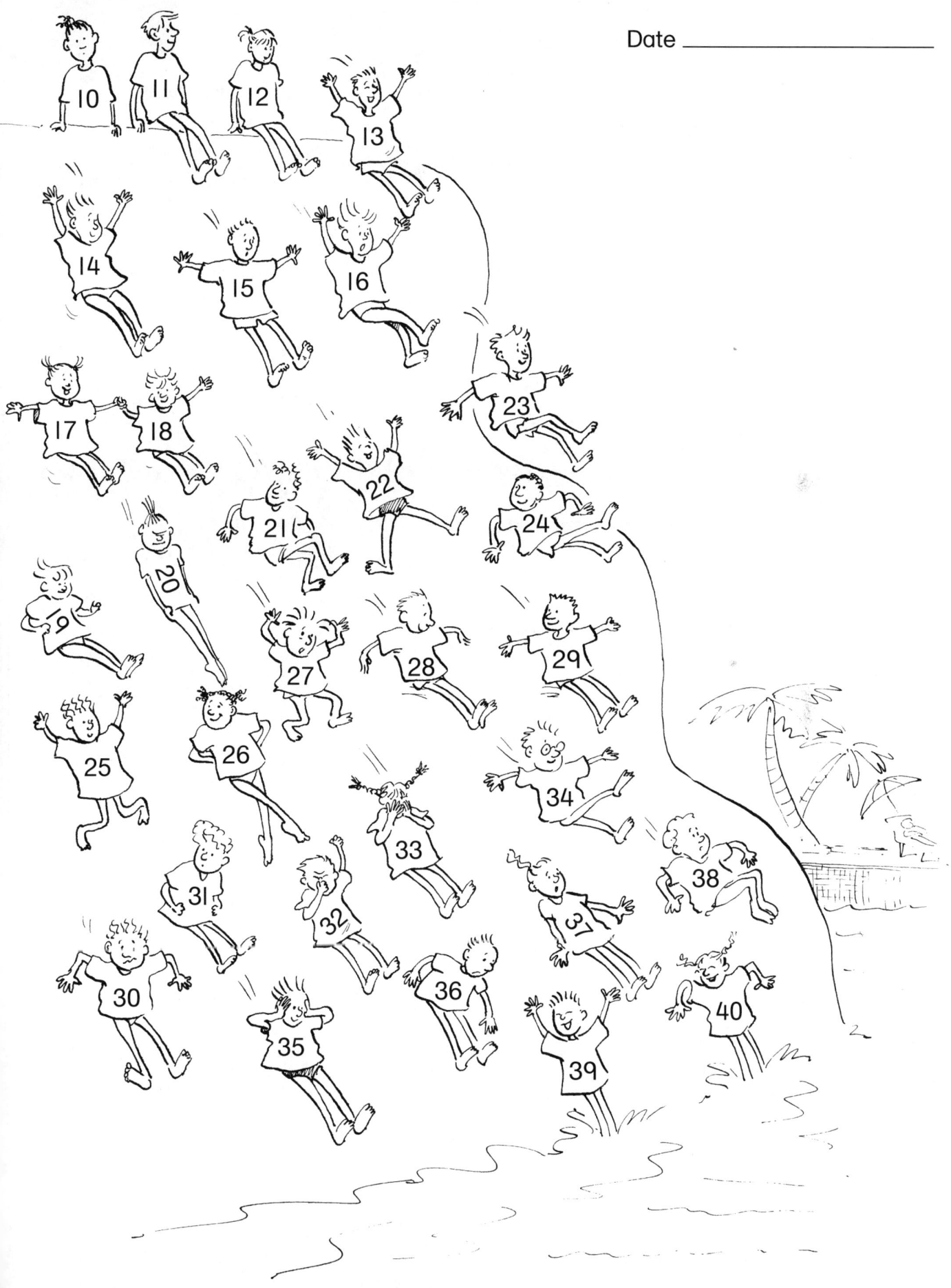

Date _____

Collins New Primary Maths: Speaking and Listening 4 © HarperCollins*Publishers* Ltd 2009

Activity 21

Year 4 Calculating

- Develop and use written methods to record, support and explain division of two-digit numbers by a one-digit number, including division with remainders.

Resources
Provide each child with the following:
- a copy of Activity 21 pupil sheet
- a red, blue, green and yellow coloured pencil

Key words
zero, one, two…one thousand   divided by   divided into

Say to the children:
Listen carefully.
I am going to tell you some things to do.
I will say them only once, so listen very carefully.
Do only the things you are told to do and nothing else.
If you make a mistake, cross it out. Do not use an eraser.
There are 6 parts to this activity.

The activity

1. What is 96 divided by six? Find that tie and colour it red.

2. What is 83 divided by three? Find that tie and colour it blue.

3. What is 76 divided by four? Find that tie and colour it yellow.

4. What is 94 divided by seven? Find that tie and colour it green

5. What is 73 divided by five? Find that tie and draw a ring around it.

6. What is 79 divided by three? Find that tie and write your name under it.

Answers

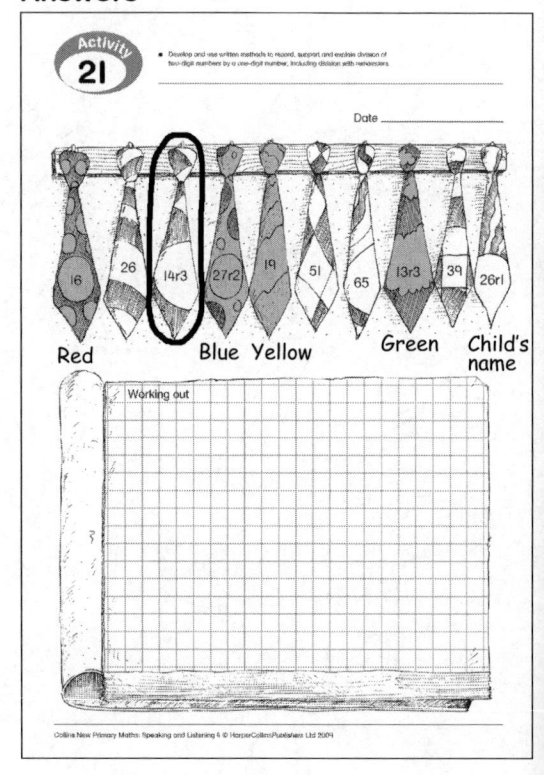

Discussion questions

↓ Which tie did you colour blue? (27r2)

↓ What did you do to the tie with the number nineteen on it? (coloured it yellow)

■ Look at one of the calculations you worked out. What is it? What is the answer? How did you work it out? Did anyone work that calculation out using a different method?

■ Who answered a calculation incorrectly? Do you know why? Where did you make a mistake?

↑ Choose a number you did not colour and divide it by three/four/five….

↑ Did you work out any of these calculations in your head? Which ones? How did you work it out? Did anyone work it out a different way?

Activity 21

- Develop and use written methods to record, support and explain division of two-digit numbers by a one-digit number, including division with remainders.

Date _____

16   26   14r3   27r2   19   51   65   13r3   39   26r1

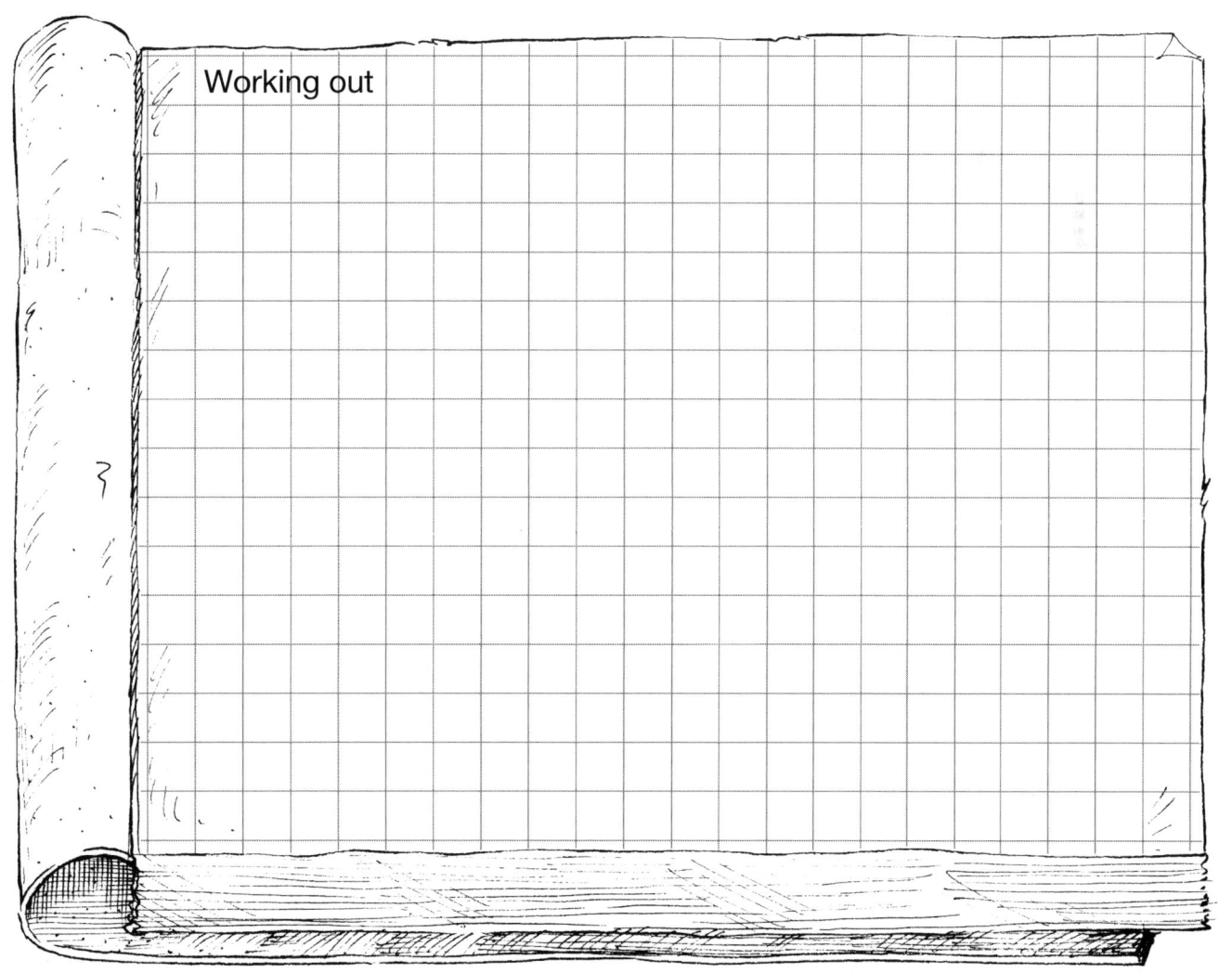

Working out

Activity 22

Year 4 Understanding shape

- Draw polygons and classify them by identifying their properties, including their line symmetry.
- Visualise 3-D objects from 2-D drawings.

Resources
Provide each child with the following:
- a copy of Activity 22 pupil sheet
- a red, blue, green, yellow, orange and purple coloured pencil

Key words
3-D (three dimensional) cube cuboid sphere cylinder pentagon heptagon cone triangular-based pyramid square-based pyramid 2-D (two dimensional) square rectangle circle equilateral triangle isosceles triangle hexagon octagon hemi-sphere tetrahedron quadrilateral

Say to the children:
Listen carefully.
I am going to tell you some things to do.
I will say them only once, so listen very carefully.
Do only the things you are told to do and nothing else.
If you make a mistake, cross it out. Do not use an eraser.
There are 16 parts to this activity.

The activity

1. Look at all the shapes. Colour the cube red.
2. Colour the pentagon blue.
3. Colour the heptagon green.
4. Colour the square-based pyramid yellow.
5. Colour the square blue.
6. Colour the cone purple.
7. Write your name inside the cuboid.
8. Write your age inside the equilateral triangle.
9. Colour the sphere red.
10. Colour the octagon orange.
11. Colour the isosceles triangle green.
12. Colour the hemi-sphere yellow.
13. Colour the rectangle orange.
14. Colour the cylinder purple.
15. Draw a cross inside the triangular-based pyramid.
16. Draw a ring around all the three dimensional shapes.

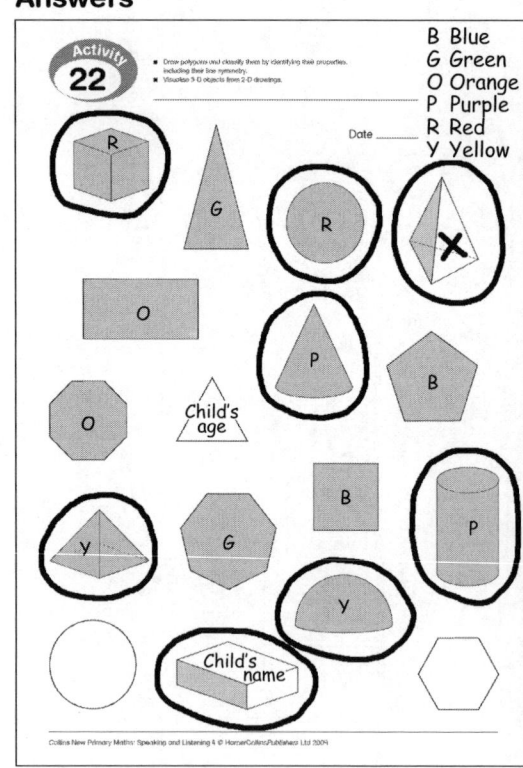

Discussion questions

- ↓ Which shape did you write your name in? (cuboid)
- ↓ Choose a shape on the sheet and name it.
- ■ Choose a shape on the sheet and describe it to me.
- ■ Look at the two triangles. What is the same/different about these triangles? What are they called? (equilateral triangle and isosceles triangle)
- ↑ What did you do to the tetrahedron? (drew a cross inside it) What is another name for this shape? (triangular-based pyramid)
- ↑ How many polygons are on the sheet? (8) What do we call any four-sided polygon? (quadrilateral)

Activity 22

- Draw polygons and classify them by identifying their properties, including their line symmetry.
- Visualise 3-D objects from 2-D drawings.

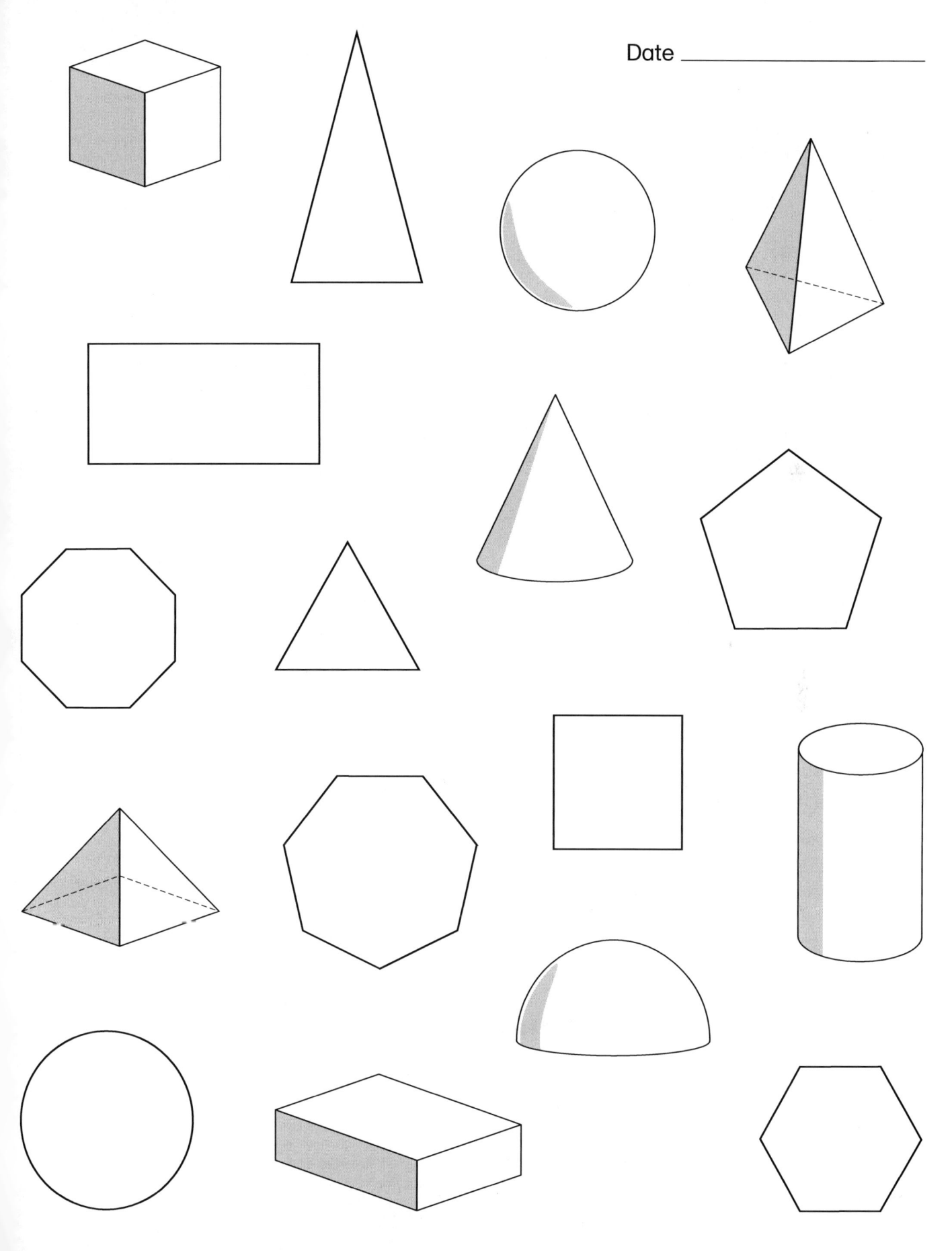

Date _____

Activity 23

Year 4 Understanding shape

- Use the eight compass points to describe direction.

Resources
Provide each child with the following:
- a copy of Activity 23 pupil sheet
- a red, blue, green and yellow coloured pencil

Key words
direction   compass   directly   north   south   east   west
north-east   south-east   south-west   north-west

Say to the children:
Listen carefully.
I am going to tell you some things to do.
I will say them only once, so listen very carefully.
Do only the things you are told to do and nothing else.
If you make a mistake, cross it out. Do not use an eraser.
There are 11 parts to this activity.

The activity

1. Look at house M. Which house is directly south of house M? Colour that house red.
2. Look at house L. Which house is directly east of house L? Colour that house blue.
3. Look at house D. Which house is directly north of house D? Colour that house green.
4. Look at house K. Which house is directly west of house K? Colour that house yellow.
5. Look at house O. Which house is directly south-east of house O? Colour that house red.
6. Look at house J. Which house is directly north-east of house J? Colour that house blue.
7. Look at house Z. Which house is directly north-west of house Z? Colour that house green.
8. Look at house M. Which house is directly south-west of house M? Colour that house yellow.
9. In which direction is house W from house Q? Circle that direction on the compass.
10. In which direction is house I from house P? Circle that direction on the compass.
11. Write your name on the house that is directly south of house U.

Answers

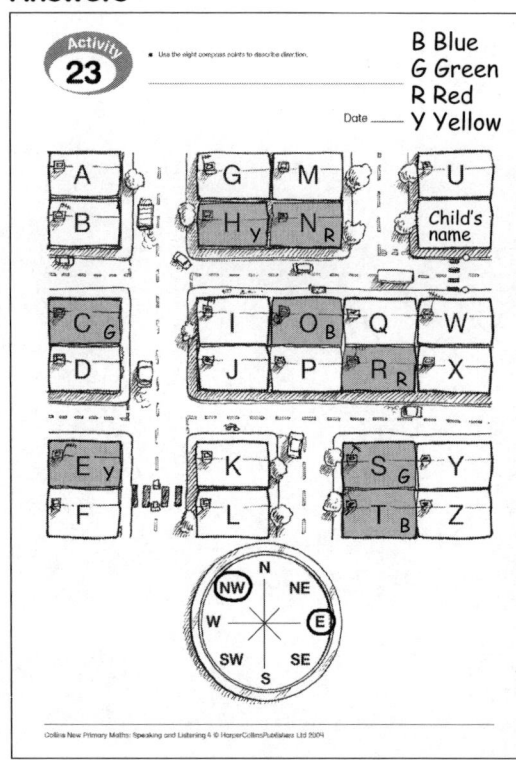

(Pupil sheet shows: B Blue, G Green, R Red, Y Yellow. Coloured houses: C G, H Y, N R, O B, E Y, R R, S G, T B)

Discussion questions

↓ Tell me a house you coloured red. (N or R)

↓ What colour is house E? (yellow)

■ Look at house L. Which house is directly east of house L? (T)

■ Look at house O. Which house is directly south-east of house O? (R)

↑ In which direction is house I from house P? (NW)

↑ Choose any two homes and tell me the direction one is from the other.

56

Activity 23

- Use the eight compass points to describe direction.

Date _____

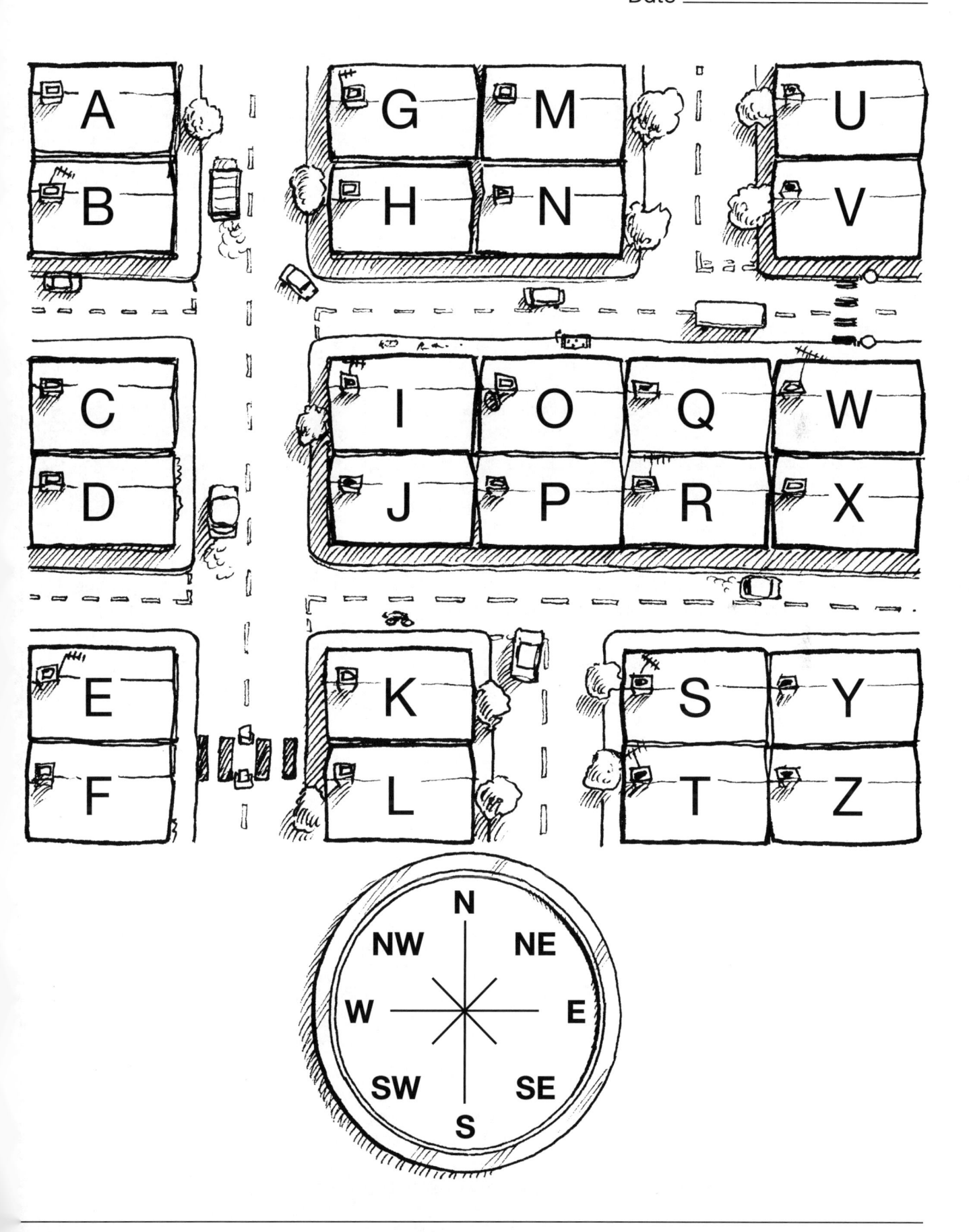

Activity 24

Year 4 Measuring

- Choose and use standard metric units and their abbreviations when estimating, measuring and recording length.
- Solve one-step and two-step problems involving measures.

Resources
Provide each child with the following:
- a copy of Activity 24 pupil sheet
- a pencil

Key words
zero, one, two… ten thousand   fabric   material   stock list
millimetres   centimetres   metres   most   least

Say to the children:
Listen carefully.
I am going to tell you some things to do.
I will say them only once, so listen very carefully.
Do only the things you are told to do and nothing else.
If you make a mistake, cross it out. Do not use an eraser.
There are 13 parts to this activity.

The activity

1. Look at *Fiona's Fabrics*. Fiona has worked out how much fabric she has left for each roll, from A to E. She has measured the rolls in centimetres only. For each roll work out how much she has in metres and centimetres. Write the answers on Fiona's stock list. Roll A has been done for you.

2. Look at *Martin's Materials*. Martin has worked out how much material he has left for each roll, from F to J. He has measured the rolls in metres and centimetres. For each roll, work out how much he has in centimetres only. Write the answers on Martin's stock list. Roll F has been done for you.

3. Look at Fiona's stock list. Draw a ring around the fabric that Fiona has the most of.

4. Look at Fiona's stock list again. Draw a star beside the fabric that Fiona has the least of.

5. Look at Martin's stock list. Draw a ring around the material that Martin has the most of.

6. Look at Martin's stock list again. Draw a star beside the material that Martin has the least of.

7. How much fabric is there altogether in rolls C and E? Write the answer in metres and centimetres, under the pair of scissors.

8. How much material is there altogether in rolls G and H? Write the answer in millimetres only, under the tape measure.

9. How much more fabric is there in roll B than in roll C? Write the answer in metres and centimetres, under the pins.

10. How much more material is there in roll J than in roll G? Write the answer in centimetres only, under the buttons.

11. How much fabric is there altogether in rolls C, D and E? Write the answer in metres and centimetres, under the reel of thread.

12. How much more material is there in roll I than in roll F? Write the answer in millimetres only under the thimble.

13. Write your name under the date.

Answers

Discussion questions

↓ Which rolls did you draw a ring around? (B and I)
↓ Did anyone write their name at the bottom of the sheet beside the word 'Name'? Were you told to? (no)
■ How many metres and centimetres are there in 530 centimetres? (5 m 30 cm)
■ How many centimetres are there in six metres and 50 centimetres? (650 cm) How many millimetres is that? (6500 mm)
↑ How many centimetres are there altogether in rolls C, D and E? (940 cm) How many metres and centimetres are there altogether in rolls C, D and E? (9 m 40 cm) How did you get that answer? How many millimetres is that? (9400 mm) How did you get that answer?
↑ How much more material is there in roll I than in roll J? (1m 60 cm/160 cm/1600 mm) How did you work it out?

Activity 24

- Choose and use standard metric units and their abbreviations when estimating, measuring and recording length.
- Solve one-step and two-step problems involving measures.

Date _____

Fiona's Fabrics
- A: 690 cm
- B: 840 cm
- C: 530 cm
- D: 100 cm
- E: 310 cm

Martin's Materials
- F: 5 m 70 cm
- G: 2 m 30 cm
- H: 4 m 20 cm
- I: 8 m 10 cm
- J: 6 m 50 cm

Fiona's Fabrics
Stock List
A **6 m 90 cm**

B _____

C _____

D _____

E _____

Martin's Materials
Stock List
F **570 cm**

G _____

H _____

I _____

J _____

Name _____

Activity 25

Year 4 Measuring

- Choose and use standard metric units and their abbreviations when estimating, measuring and recording mass.
- Solve one-step and two-step problems involving measures.

Resources
Provide each child with the following:
- a copy of Activity 25 pupil sheet
- a pencil

Key words
zero, one, two… ten thousand weigh weight kilograms
grams difference altogether

Say to the children:
Listen carefully.
I am going to tell you some things to do.
I will say them only once, so listen very carefully.
Do only the things you are told to do and nothing else.
If you make a mistake, cross it out. Do not use an eraser.
There are 14 parts to this activity.

The activity

1. At the airport, some check-in counters have weighed the parcels in kilograms and grams, and others have weighed them in grams only. Help Sam to convert the weights of the parcels by writing the answers on the parcel weight form. Sam has done the first one for you.

2. How much do the parcels going to Berlin and Rome weigh altogether? Write the answer in grams only on check-in one.

3. How much do the parcels going to New York and Sydney weigh altogether? Write the answer in kilograms and grams on check-in two.

4. What is the difference in weight between the parcels going to Delhi and Hong Kong? Write the answer in grams and kilograms on check-in three.

5. What is the difference in weight between the parcels going to Washington and Tokyo? Write the answer in grams only on check-in four.

6. How much do the parcels going to New York and Moscow weigh altogether? Write the answer in grams only on check-in five.

7. How much do the parcels going to Washington and Rome weigh altogether? Write the answer in kilograms and grams on check-in six.

8. What is the difference in weight between the parcels going to Berlin and Paris? Write the answer in grams and kilograms on check-in seven.

9. What is the difference in weight between the parcels going to Delhi and Moscow? Write the answer in grams only on check-in eight.

10. How much do the parcels going to Hong Kong and Paris weigh altogether? Write the answer in kilograms and grams on check-in nine.

11. What is the difference in weight between the parcels going to Paris and New York? Write the answer in kilograms and grams on check-in ten.

12. How much do the parcels going to Tokyo and Delhi weigh altogether? Write the answer in grams only on check-in eleven.

13. What is the difference in weight between the parcels going to Rome and New York? Write the answer in grams only on check-in twelve.

14. Write your name beside Sam.

Answers

Discussion questions

↓ Where is the heaviest/lightest parcel travelling to? (Sydney/Rome)

↓ Which parcel weighs 2300 g? (parcel going to New York)

■ What is the difference in weight between the parcels going to Paris and New York? (2 kg 500 g/2500 g)

■ How much do the parcels going to Washington and Rome weigh altogether? (8 kg 900 g/8900 g)

↑ How many parcels weigh more than five kilograms? (5) Where are they going? (Berlin, Sydney, Moscow, Washington, Delhi)

↑ What is the total weight of the parcels going to New York, Moscow and Tokyo? (11 kg 800 g/11 800 g)

60

Activity 25

- Choose and use standard metric units and their abbreviations when estimating, measuring and recording mass.
- Solve one-step and two-step problems involving measures.

Date _____

PARCEL WEIGHT FORM

	g	kg / g
Paris	4800 g	4 kg 800 g
Berlin	7000 g	_____
New York	_____	2 kg 300 g
Sydney	_____	9 kg 200 g
Rome	1600 g	_____
Moscow	_____	5 kg 400 g
Washington	7300 g	_____
Hong Kong	_____	3 kg 500 g
Tokyo	4100 g	_____
Delhi	_____	5 kg 700 g

Collins New Primary Maths: Speaking and Listening 4 © HarperCollins*Publishers* Ltd 2009

Activity 26

Year 4 Measuring

- Choose and use standard metric units and their abbreviations when estimating, measuring and recording capacity.
- Solve one-step and two-step problems involving measures.

Resources
Provide each child with the following:
- a copy of Activity 26 pupil sheet
- a pencil

Key words
zero, one, two… ten thousand litres millilitres containers convert how much? how much more?

Say to the children:
Listen carefully.

I am going to tell you some things to do.

I will say them only once, so listen very carefully.

Do only the things you are told to do and nothing else.

If you make a mistake, cross it out. Do not use an eraser.

There are 14 parts to this activity.

The activity

1. Michael Thomson is a farmer. The containers that are used to store milk use litres and millilitres. The containers that are used to store cream and yoghurt use millilitres only. Help Michael to convert his dairy products so that he can easily work out how much milk, cream and yoghurt he has. Michael has done the first one for you.
2. How much full cream milk and semi-skimmed milk does Michael have altogether? Write the answer in litres and millilitres in box one.
3. How much semi-skimmed milk and skimmed milk does Michael have altogether? Write the answer in litres and millilitres in box two.
4. How much single cream and double cream does Michael have altogether? Write the answer in millilitres only in box three.
5. How much double cream and yoghurt does Michael have altogether? Write the answer in millilitres only in box four.
6. How much full cream milk and skimmed milk does Michael have altogether? Write the answer in millilitres only in box five.
7. How much single cream and yoghurt does Michael have altogether? Write the answer in litres and millilitres in box six.
8. How much semi-skimmed milk and single cream does Michael have altogether? Write the answer in millilitres only in box seven.
9. How much milk does Michael have altogether? Write the answer in litres and millilitres in box eight.
10. How much more semi-skimmed milk than skimmed milk does Michael have? Write the answer in litres and millilitres in box nine.
11. How much more full cream milk than yoghurt does Michael have? Write the answer in millilitres only in box ten.
12. How much more yoghurt than single cream does Michael have? Write the answer in litres and millilitres in box eleven.
13. How much more skimmed milk than double cream does Michael have? Write the answer in millilitres only in box twelve.
14. Write your name at the top of the sheet.

Answers

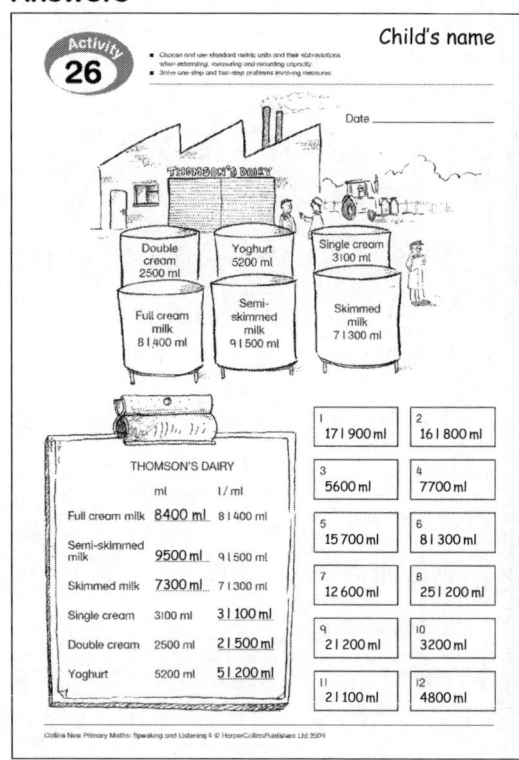

Child's name

Date _____

THOMSON'S DAIRY

- Double cream 2500 ml
- Yoghurt 5200 ml
- Single cream 3100 ml
- Full cream milk 8 l 400 ml
- Semi-skimmed milk 9 l 500 ml
- Skimmed milk 7 l 300 ml

THOMSON'S DAIRY

	ml	l / ml
Full cream milk	8400 ml	8 l 400 ml
Semi-skimmed milk	9500 ml	9 l 500 ml
Skimmed milk	7300 ml	7 l 300 ml
Single cream	3100 ml	3 l 100 ml
Double cream	2500 ml	2 l 500 ml
Yoghurt	5200 ml	5 l 200 ml

1	2
17 l 900 ml	16 l 800 ml
3	4
5600 ml	7700 ml
5	6
15 700 ml	8 l 300 ml
7	8
12 600 ml	25 l 200 ml
9	10
2 l 200 ml	3200 ml
11	12
2 l 100 ml	4800 ml

Discussion questions

↓ What did you write in box three? (5600 ml) What is that in litres and millilitres? (5 l 600 ml)

↓ What product does Michael have most/least of? (semi-skimmed milk/double cream)

■ How much more yoghurt than single cream does Michael have? (2 l 100 ml/2100 ml) Where did you write that answer? (box 11)

■ How much milk does Michael have altogether? (25 l 200 ml/25 200 ml) Where did you write that answer? (box 8)

↑ How much milk, cream and yoghurt does Michael have altogether? (36 0 l)

↑ Three months later, Michael's farm produced twice as much milk. How much milk is that altogether? (50 l 400 ml/50 400 ml) However, he only produced half as much cream and yoghurt. How much is that? (5 l 400 ml/5400 ml)

Activity 26

- Choose and use standard metric units and their abbreviations when estimating, measuring and recording capacity.
- Solve one-step and two-step problems involving measures.

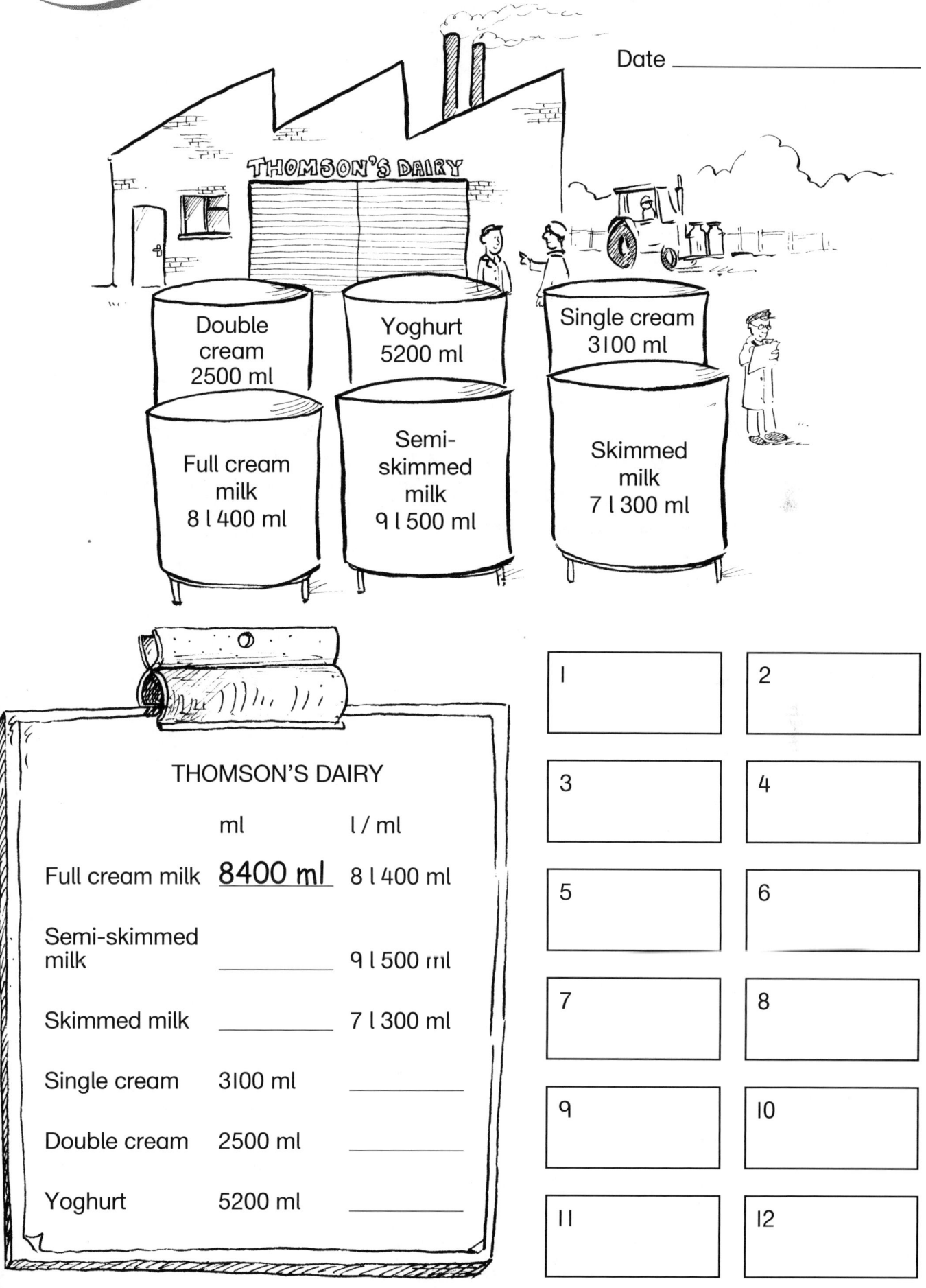

Date _____

Containers at Thomson's Dairy:
- Double cream 2500 ml
- Yoghurt 5200 ml
- Single cream 3100 ml
- Full cream milk 8 l 400 ml
- Semi-skimmed milk 9 l 500 ml
- Skimmed milk 7 l 300 ml

THOMSON'S DAIRY

	ml	l / ml
Full cream milk	**8400 ml**	8 l 400 ml
Semi-skimmed milk	_____	9 l 500 ml
Skimmed milk	_____	7 l 300 ml
Single cream	3100 ml	_____
Double cream	2500 ml	_____
Yoghurt	5200 ml	_____

1	2
3	4
5	6
7	8
9	10
11	12

Activity 27

Year 4 Measuring

- Draw rectangles and measure and calculate their perimeters; find the area of rectilinear shapes drawn on a square grid by counting squares.

Resources
Provide each child with the following:
- a copy of Activity 27 pupil sheet
- a red, blue, green and yellow coloured pencil
- a pencil

Key words
zero, one, two…one hundred   area   perimeter   centimetres   square centimetres   above   below

Say to the children:
Listen carefully.
I am going to tell you some things to do.
I will say them only once, so listen very carefully.
Do only the things you are told to do and nothing else.
If you make a mistake, cross it out. Do not use an eraser.
There are 12 parts to this activity.

The activity

1. Look at shape A. What is the area of shape A? Write the answer under the shape.
2. Look at shape B. What is the perimeter of shape B? Write the answer above the shape.
3. Which shape has an area of 12 square centimetres? Colour that shape red.
4. Which shape has a perimeter of 28 centimetres? Colour that shape blue.
5. Look at shape C. What is the area of shape C? Write the answer under the shape.
6. Look at shape E. What is the perimeter of shape E? Write the answer under the shape.
7. Which shape has an area of 30 square centimetres? Colour that shape green.
8. Which shape has a perimeter of 22 centimetres? Colour that shape yellow.
9. Look at shape D. What is the area of shape D? Write the answer under the shape.
10. Look at shape F. What is the perimeter of shape F? Write the answer above the shape.
11. Which shape has an area of 63 square centimetres? Write your name inside that shape.
12. Which shape has a perimeter of 20 centimetres? Write the answer inside that shape.

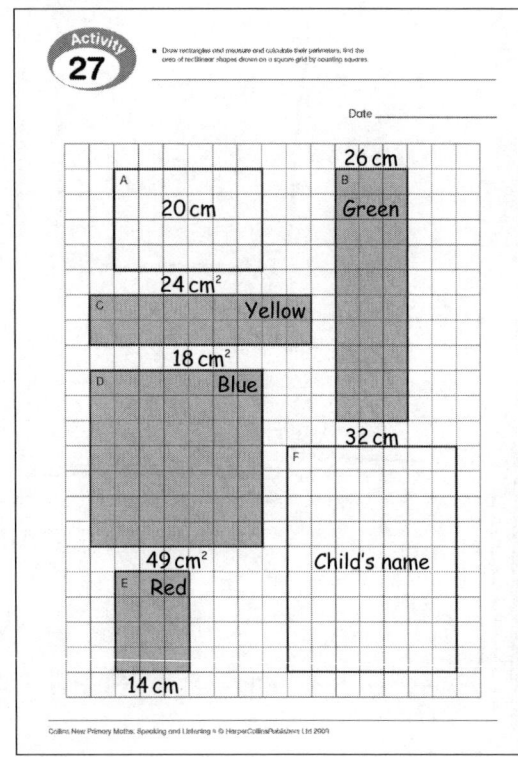

Discussion questions

↓ Which shape did you colour red? (E)

↓ Choose any shape and tell me the area/perimeter of that shape.

■ What is the perimeter of shape A? (20cm) What is the area of shape A? (24cm^2)

■ Which shapes have got a perimeter greater than 24 centimetres? (B, D, F)

↑ Which shape has the largest/smallest area? (F/E) Which shape has the largest/smallest perimeter? (F/E)

↑ Look at the area of each shape. Tell me the shapes in order of size, from smallest to largest. (E, C, A, B, D, F)

Activity 27

- Draw rectangles and measure and calculate their perimeters; find the area of rectilinear shapes drawn on a square grid by counting squares.

Date _____

Activity 28

Year 4 Measuring

- Read time to the nearest minute; use am, pm and 12-hour clock notation.

Resources
Provide each child with the following:
- a copy of Activity 28 pupil sheet
- a red, blue, green and yellow coloured pencil

Key words
zero, one, two…sixty clock o'clock time morning afternoon evening night minute past to half past quarter to/quarter past

Say to the children:
Listen carefully.

I am going to tell you some things to do.

I will say them only once, so listen very carefully.

Do only the things you are told to do and nothing else.

If you make a mistake, cross it out. Do not use an eraser.

There are 12 parts to this activity.

The activity

1. To show am or pm on the digital clocks, you must colour the appropriate circle. Find the clock that reads two minutes past five. Write your name under that clock.
2. Look at clock I. Show the time of twenty minutes past ten in the evening.
3. Look at clock E. Show the time of nine minutes past eight.
4. Find the clock that reads four minutes past seven. Colour that clock red.
5. Look at clock C. Show the time of quarter to eleven in the morning.
6. Look at clock K. Show the time of eighteen minutes to two.
7. Find the clock that reads half past three in the morning. Colour that clock blue.
8. Look at clock A. Show the time of seventeen minutes past nine.
9. Look at clock G. Show the time of twenty-nine minutes past twelve in the afternoon.
10. Find the clock that reads thirty-four minutes past one. Colour that clock green.
11. Look at clock D. Show the time of five minutes to two in the afternoon.
12. Find the clock that reads three thirty in the afternoon. Colour that clock yellow.

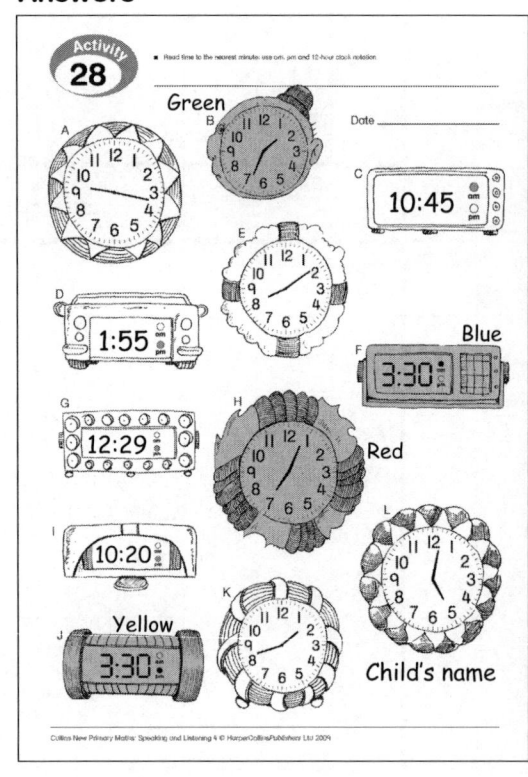

Discussion questions

↓ Which clock shows the time of quarter to eleven? (C)

↓ What time does clock J read? (3:30 pm)

■ Choose a clock and tell me the time. Can you say this time another way?

■ What do you notice about clocks F and J? (They show the same time in the morning and afternoon.)

↑ What is the difference in time between clocks B and G? (1 hour 5 minutes)

↑ Imagine the time is now half past one. Which clock shows what time it will be in twelve minutes' time? (K) What time is that? (18 minutes to 2)

Activity 28

■ Read time to the nearest minute; use am, pm and 12-hour clock notation.

Date _____

A

B

C

D

E

F 3:30 pm

G

H

I

J 3:30 pm

K

L

Activity 29

Year 4 Measuring

- Calculate time intervals using a calendar.

Resources
Provide each child with the following:
- a copy of Activity 29 pupil sheet
- a coloured pencil
- a pencil

Key words
time   calendar   date   day   Monday, Tuesday, Wednesday… Sunday   week   month   January, February, March… December   year

Say to the children:
Listen carefully.
I am going to tell you some things to do.
I will say them only once, so listen very carefully.
Do only the things you are told to do and nothing else.
If you make a mistake, cross it out. Do not use an eraser.
There are 15 parts to this activity.

The activity

1. Which day of the week is the first of August? Write that day on note number one.

2. How many Fridays are there in October? Write the answer on note number two.

3. Using your coloured pencil, colour the week beginning Monday the 13th of May.

4. Which day of the week is the last day in July? Write that day on note number three.

5. How many days are there in February? Write the answer on note number four.

6. Which day of the week is the 29th of September? Write that day on note number five.

7. What is the date of the third Thursday in March? Write that day on note number six.

8. Using your coloured pencil, colour all the Mondays in April.

9. How many days are there from the 28th of May to the 6th of June? Write the answer on note number seven.

10. How many weeks are there from the 11th of September to the 23rd of October? Write the answer on note number eight.

11. Which day of the week is the 13th of December? Write that day on note number nine.

12. Using your coloured pencil, colour the 18th of July.

13. Write your name on note number ten.

14. How many days are there from the 24th of January to the 17th of February? Write the answer on note number eleven.

15. How many weeks are there from the 12th of June to the 14th of August? Write the answer on note number twelve.

Answers

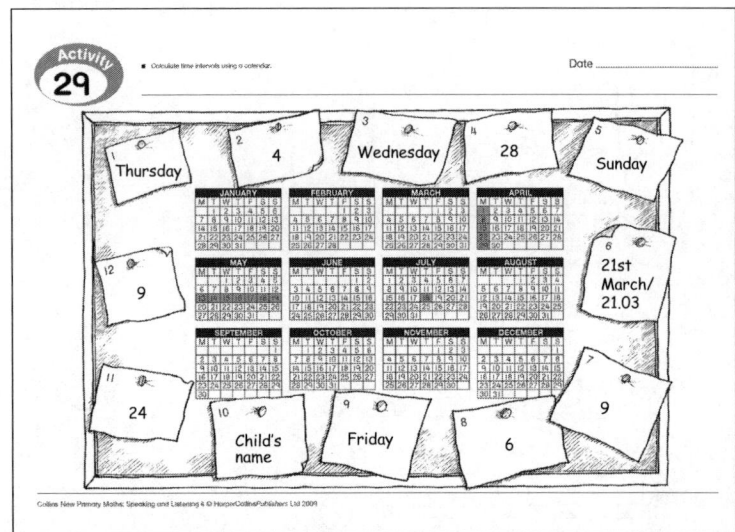

Discussion questions

↓ What did you write on note number three? (Wednesday)

↓ How many days are there in February? (28)

■ Which day of the week is the 19th of September? (Thursday)

■ How many days are there from the 24th of January to the 17th of February? (24) Where did you write that answer? (note 11)

↑ How many weeks are there from the 12th of June to the 14th of August? (9)

↑ According to this calendar, which day of the week is it today/does your birthday fall/is Christmas?

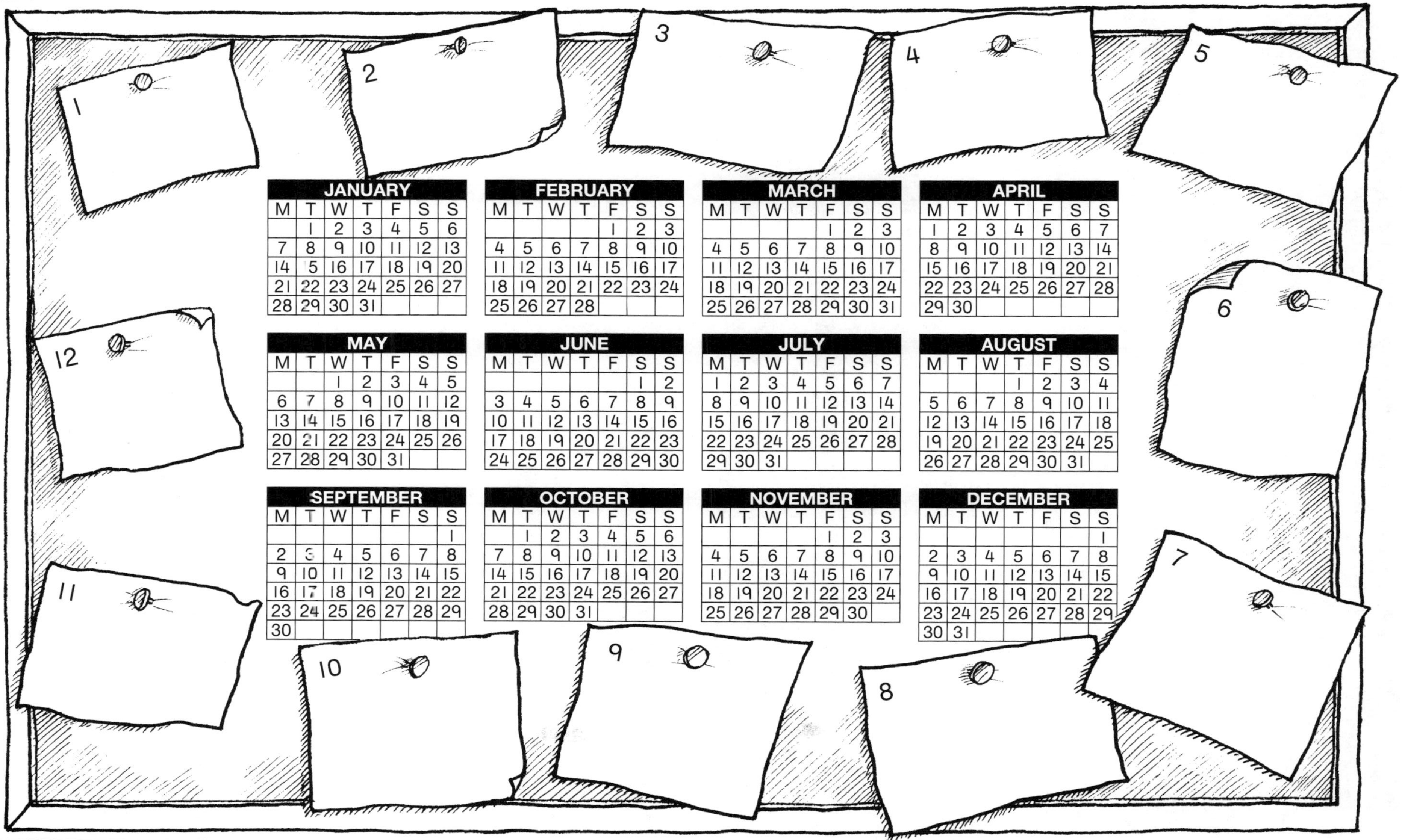

Date _____

- Calculate time intervals using a calendar.

Activity 29

JANUARY								FEBRUARY								MARCH								APRIL						
M	T	W	T	F	S	S		M	T	W	T	F	S	S		M	T	W	T	F	S	S		M	T	W	T	F	S	S
	1	2	3	4	5	6						1	2	3						1	2	3		1	2	3	4	5	6	7
7	8	9	10	11	12	13		4	5	6	7	8	9	10		4	5	6	7	8	9	10		8	9	10	11	12	13	14
14	15	16	17	18	19	20		11	12	13	14	15	16	17		11	12	13	14	15	16	17		15	16	17	18	19	20	21
21	22	23	24	25	26	27		18	19	20	21	22	23	24		18	19	20	21	22	23	24		22	23	24	25	26	27	28
28	29	30	31					25	26	27	28					25	26	27	28	29	30	31		29	30					

MAY								JUNE								JULY								AUGUST						
M	T	W	T	F	S	S		M	T	W	T	F	S	S		M	T	W	T	F	S	S		M	T	W	T	F	S	S
		1	2	3	4	5							1	2		1	2	3	4	5	6	7					1	2	3	4
6	7	8	9	10	11	12		3	4	5	6	7	8	9		8	9	10	11	12	13	14		5	6	7	8	9	10	11
13	14	15	16	17	18	19		10	11	12	13	14	15	16		15	16	17	18	19	20	21		12	13	14	15	16	17	18
20	21	22	23	24	25	26		17	18	19	20	21	22	23		22	23	24	25	26	27	28		19	20	21	22	23	24	25
27	28	29	30	31				24	25	26	27	28	29	30		29	30	31						26	27	28	29	30	31	

SEPTEMBER								OCTOBER								NOVEMBER								DECEMBER						
M	T	W	T	F	S	S		M	T	W	T	F	S	S		M	T	W	T	F	S	S		M	T	W	T	F	S	S
						1			1	2	3	4	5	6						1	2	3								1
2	3	4	5	6	7	8		7	8	9	10	11	12	13		4	5	6	7	8	9	10		2	3	4	5	6	7	8
9	10	11	12	13	14	15		14	15	16	17	18	19	20		11	12	13	14	15	16	17		9	10	11	12	13	14	15
16	17	18	19	20	21	22		21	22	23	24	25	26	27		18	19	20	21	22	23	24		16	17	18	19	20	21	22
23	24	25	26	27	28	29		28	29	30	31					25	26	27	28	29	30			23	24	25	26	27	28	29
30																								30	31					

Activity 30

Year 4 Handling data

- Answer a question by identifying what data to collect; organise, present, analyse and interpret the data in diagrams (e.g. Venn and Carroll diagrams).

Resources

Provide each child with the following:
- a copy of Activity 30 pupil sheet
- a pencil

You will also need 30 randomly selected playing cards (picture cards removed), shuffled and placed face down in a pile.

Key words

zero, one, two…ten   Venn diagram   Carroll diagram

Say to the children:

Listen carefully.

I am going to tell you some things to do.

I will say them only once, so listen very carefully.

Do only the things you are told to do and nothing else.

If you make a mistake, cross it out. Do not use an eraser.

There are 32 parts to this activity.

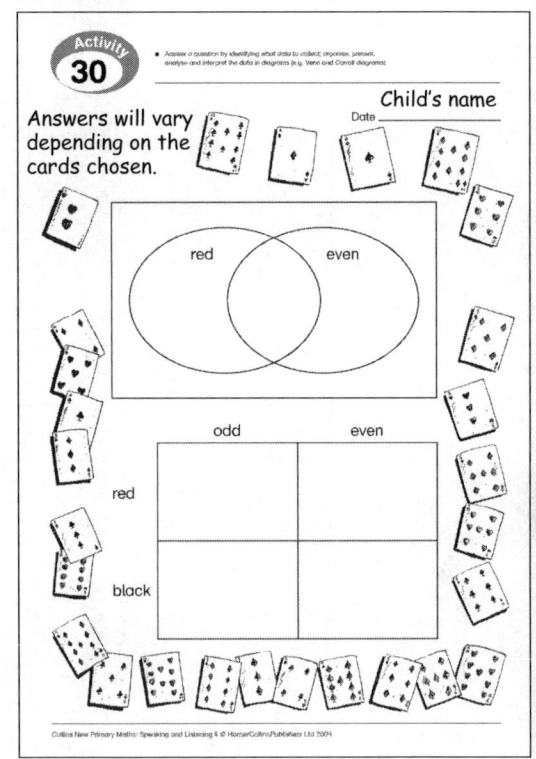

The activity

Note: Italicised instructions are for the teacher and are not to be read out to the children.

1. Write your name above the date.

2. This activity is about collecting and organising data in Venn and Carroll diagrams.
   I am going to choose a card and call out the number and the colour. Each time I call out the number and colour, you have to write that number in the appropriate place on both the Venn and Carroll diagrams.

3 – 32. *Choose a card and call out the number and colour. Continue until all thirty cards have been chosen.*

Discussion questions

↓ How many of the cards chosen were even?

↓ Which colour was chosen the most?

■ How many cards were black and odd/black and even/red and odd/red and even?

■ Altogether how many cards did I choose? (30)

↑ What do you notice about the Venn and Carroll diagram? (They contain the same information.)

↑ Are there more odd numbers or even numbers? How many more?

Answers

Answers will vary depending on the cards chosen.

Activity 30

- Answer a question by identifying what data to collect; organise, present, analyse and interpret the data in diagrams (e.g. Venn and Carroll diagrams).

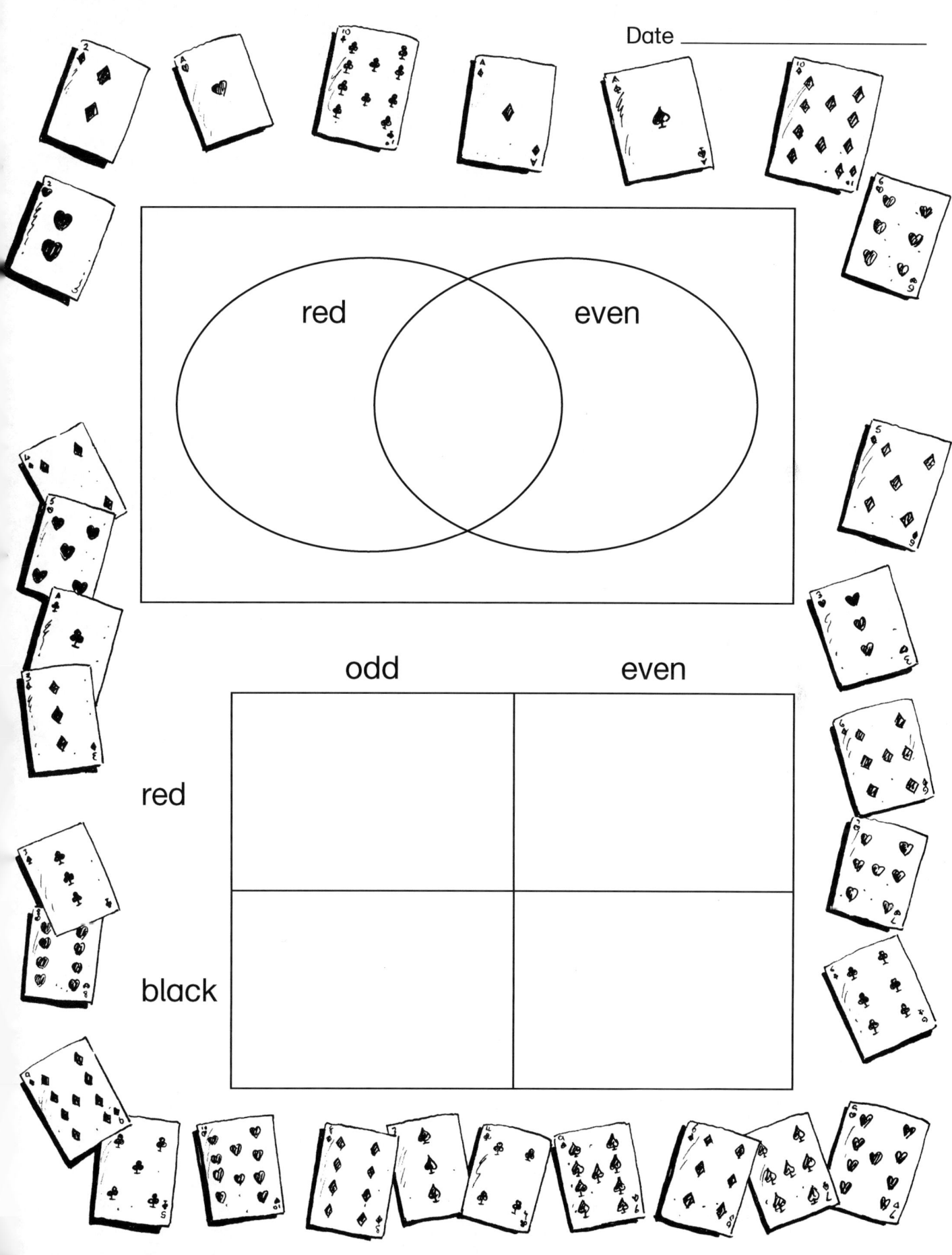

Date _____

red   even

odd   even

red

black

Collins New Primary Maths: Speaking and Listening 4 © HarperCollinsPublishers Ltd 2009